TypeScript for Beginners

A Beginner's Guide to the Future of
JavaScript

Adriam Miller

Discover Other Books in the Series

"TypeScript for Backend Development: Backend applications with Node.js, Express, and modern frameworks"

"TypeScript for Blockchain: Unlock the full potential of TypeScript in Web3 development"

"TypeScript for DevOps: The Secret Weapon for Automating, Scaling, and Securing Your Infrastructure"

"Typescript for Front End Development: Reduce Errors, Boost Productivity, and Master Modern Web Development Like a Pro"

"TypeScript for JavaScript Developers: The Essential Guide for JavaScript Developers to Write Safer, Scalable, and More Efficient Code"

"Typescript for Microservices: Learn How to Leverage TypeScript to Develop Robust, Maintainable, and Efficient Microservices Architecture"

"TypeScript for Mobile Application Development: Build Faster, Safer, and Smarter Applications with Ease"

"TypeScript for Web Development: Boost Your Productivity, Eliminate Costly Errors, and Build Scalable Web Applications with TypeScript"

Disclaimer

The information provided in this book, **"TypeScript for Beginners: A Beginner's Guide to the Future of JavaScript"** by **Adrian Miller**, is for **educational and informational purposes only**. The content is designed to help readers understand TypeScript programming.

Introduction

Welcome to TypeScript for Beginners: A Beginner's Guide to the Future of JavaScript. In recent years, JavaScript has solidified its position as a fundamental element of web development, facilitating everything from dynamic websites to robust backend systems. However, as projects increase in complexity, developers encounter difficulties in navigating the nuances of the language. This is where TypeScript becomes essential—a powerful superset of JavaScript that incorporates static typing, contemporary features, and a more organized coding methodology.

This book is tailored for you, whether you are entirely new to programming or an experienced JavaScript developer seeking to refine your expertise. TypeScript presents an opportunity to produce cleaner, more maintainable code while still taking advantage of the extensive ecosystem and flexibility that JavaScript offers.

Our objective is to provide you with the knowledge and tools required to transition confidently from JavaScript to TypeScript. By the conclusion of this book, you will possess a thorough understanding of TypeScript's features and be capable of developing robust applications with improved readability and maintainability. As the programming landscape continues to evolve, TypeScript stands out as a crucial skill for developers of all levels. By embracing TypeScript, you are not only preparing yourself for current industry trends but also embracing a future where safer and more scalable web applications will dominate.

So, whether you're embarking on your coding journey or looking to refine your existing skills, dive in and discover how TypeScript can transform the way you write code. Let's get started on this exciting adventure into the future of JavaScript!

Chapter 1: Introduction to TypeScript

TypeScript, developed by Microsoft and initially launched in 2012, was designed to address the difficulties encountered by developers working on large-scale applications utilizing JavaScript. By incorporating optional static typing, TypeScript allows developers to identify errors during the compilation process instead of at runtime, thereby greatly enhancing both the development workflow and the quality of the software produced.

JavaScript, being a dynamic and loosely-typed language, provides developers with the agility to write code rapidly; however, this same flexibility can result in unforeseen behaviors and runtime errors. TypeScript mitigates these issues by providing a type system that enables developers to specify the structure of their data and the contracts of their functions. This approach not only helps in avoiding frequent programming mistakes but also enriches the overall development experience.

Key Features of TypeScript ### 1. Static Typing

A standout feature of TypeScript is its capability for static typing. In contrast to JavaScript, where type enforcement is not explicit, TypeScript permits developers to define types for variables, function parameters, and return values. This functionality improves code clarity and facilitates a better understanding of the intentions behind different segments of code. For example, consider a function that adds two numbers:

```javascript
function add(a, b) {

return a + b;
```

```
}
```

In JavaScript, if a non-numeric value is passed to this function, it will result in unexpected behavior, leading to potential bugs. In TypeScript, you can explicitly declare the argument types:

```typescript
function add(a: number, b: number): number { return a +
b;
}
```

With this type declaration, TypeScript will throw an error at compile time if non-numeric values are passed to the function.

2. Interfaces and Type Definitions

TypeScript supports the use of interfaces, which allow developers to define custom object shapes. This feature is particularly useful when working with complex data structures or when interacting with APIs. By defining an interface, you can ensure that objects adhere to a specific structure, improving consistency and reducing errors.

Here is an example of how to use interfaces in TypeScript:

```typescript
interface User {
id: number; name: string; email: string;
}
function createUser(user: User): void { console.log(`User
created: ${user.name}`);
```

```
}
const newUser = { id: 1, name: "John Doe", email:
"john@example.com" }; createUser(newUser);
```

3. Type Inference

TypeScript includes a feature called type inference, which
allows the compiler to automatically infer the type of a
variable based on its initial value. This means that you can
enjoy the benefits of type-checking without always having
to explicitly declare types for every variable.

```typescript
let message = "Hello, TypeScript"; // TypeScript infers the
type as 'string'
```

This feature not only simplifies code but also can lead to
fewer errors as the type system becomes more intuitive.

4. Compatibility with JavaScript

TypeScript is designed to be fully compatible with
JavaScript. Any valid JavaScript code is also valid
TypeScript code. This means that developers can gradually
adopt TypeScript in existing JavaScript projects without
the need for a complete rewrite. The transition to
TypeScript can be made incrementally, allowing teams to
maintain productivity while improving code quality over
time.

5. Modern Features

TypeScript also includes support for modern JavaScript
features, such as async/await, destructuring, and spread

operators. It acts as a bridge to the latest JavaScript syntax, enabling developers to take advantage of the newest features while still benefiting from the static type-checking.

Why Use TypeScript?

There are several compelling reasons to consider using TypeScript in your projects:

Error Detection: TypeScript helps catch errors early in the development process, which can save time and reduce frustration during debugging.

Improved Readability and Maintainability: The explicit nature of static types enhances code readability, making it easier for new developers to understand existing codebases.

Better Tooling: Many IDEs (such as Visual Studio Code) offer enhanced autocomplete, refactoring, and navigation capabilities for TypeScript projects, leading to a better developer experience.

Collaboration: In larger teams, the use of TypeScript can enforce a common understanding of data structures and function contracts, making it easier to collaborate and work in parallel without misunderstandings.

Community and Ecosystem: TypeScript has gained significant traction within the developer community, with a rich ecosystem of libraries, tools, and frameworks built around it. Projects like Angular, React (with TypeScript integrations), and even Node.js can benefit from TypeScript's features.

TypeScript represents a significant evolution in the way developers can work with JavaScript. By providing optional static typing and a richer tooling ecosystem, it enhances the development experience and promotes better coding practices.

TypeScript: The Future of JavaScript

JavaScript, the de facto language of the web, has been at the forefront of this evolution. However, as applications have grown in complexity, developers have faced significant challenges managing large codebases, ensuring code quality, and maintaining scalability. Enter TypeScript—a superset of JavaScript introduced by Microsoft that promises to address these challenges while enhancing the JavaScript experience. In this chapter, we will explore why TypeScript is not just a trend but represents the future of JavaScript development.

The Rise of TypeScript

TypeScript was released in 2012, but it wasn't until the late 2010s that it gained significant traction. The rise of single-page applications (SPAs) and complex front-end frameworks like Angular, React, and Vue.js catalyzed this change. Developers began to realize that the dynamic nature of JavaScript, while powerful, could lead to bugs and maintenance nightmares when scaling applications. TypeScript offered a solution by introducing static typing, which allows developers to catch errors at compile time rather than runtime.

The Power of Static Typing

At its core, TypeScript's primary feature is static typing. Unlike JavaScript, where variable types are determined at runtime, TypeScript allows developers to explicitly define types for variables, function parameters, and return values. This feature leads to several key benefits:

Early Error Detection: TypeScript catches type-related errors during the compile phase, significantly reducing the likelihood of runtime errors that can lead to application crashes or unexpected behavior in production.

Enhanced Tooling and Autocompletion: With type definitions in place, IDEs and text editors can provide better autocompletion, code navigation, and error-checking features. This experience improves developer productivity and reduces the cognitive load associated with remembering function signatures and their respective data types.

Readable and Maintainable Code: TypeScript's type annotations serve as documentation within the code itself. This leads to codebases that are easier to understand, even for developers who did not originally write the code. New team members can onboard more quickly and contribute with lower friction.

Ecosystem and Community Adoption

Although TypeScript started as a niche tool adopted primarily by large enterprises, its adoption has rapidly accelerated across the developer community. Frameworks and libraries have embraced TypeScript, with many offering first-class support. For instance, Angular is built with TypeScript, and both React and Vue.js have extensive TypeScript documentation and tooling. Additionally, libraries like Redux and RxJS provide TypeScript type definitions to fully leverage its capabilities.

The growing ecosystem has been bolstered by the active

TypeScript community, which contributes to a rich repository of third-party type definitions through DefinitelyTyped. This commitment to community-driven type definitions allows developers to incorporate TypeScript into their projects seamlessly, regardless of the libraries and tools they choose to use.

TypeScript vs. JavaScript: A Comparative Analysis

While TypeScript compiles down to plain JavaScript, it is essential to understand the differences in development experience and code outputs between the two languages. Here are some essential factors to consider:

Safety vs. Flexibility

JavaScript's flexibility allows developers to write code quickly, which can be beneficial in certain situations, especially during rapid prototyping. However, this flexibility comes at a cost—greater susceptibility to bugs and a steep learning curve for maintaining large applications. TypeScript's rigid type system introduces a safety net, encouraging developers to think critically about their data structures and interactions, ultimately leading to more robust applications.

Learning Curve

Transitioning to TypeScript can be daunting for developers accustomed to the dynamic nature of JavaScript. However, TypeScript is designed to be approachable; developers can gradually adopt static typing in existing JavaScript codebases, allowing for a smoother transition. The TypeScript compiler often offers helpful error messages and suggestions, aiding developers as they adapt their coding practices.

Industry Adoption and Case Studies

Numerous companies have already made the leap to TypeScript and reaped significant rewards. For instance, Airbnb, Slack, and Microsoft's own Office 365 have adopted TypeScript to manage their large codebases successfully. These case studies demonstrate how TypeScript can improve developer productivity and software quality, making a compelling argument for its adoption in organizations of all sizes.

Scaling Teams and Codebases

As development teams grow, coordinating changes across multiple developer efforts becomes increasingly complex. TypeScript's structured type system helps teams establish clear contracts around APIs and data structures, reducing misunderstandings and miscommunication. This standardization is crucial for scaling engineering efforts while minimizing the chances of introducing defects as projects evolve.

The Future Directions of TypeScript

The future of TypeScript looks bright, as it continues to receive significant investments from Microsoft and the developer community. Here are several directions where TypeScript is headed:

Improved Tooling

As TypeScript gains popularity, the tooling around it will continue to improve. Integrated Development Environments (IDEs) are increasingly offering better support, with features like real-time linting, seamless integration of type definitions, and improved debugging tools.

Enhancements to Type Inference

Type inference allows TypeScript to infer types where they are not explicitly defined. As TypeScript's type inference capabilities improve, developers will be able to write less code while still enjoying the benefits of strong type checking.

Server-Side Adoption

While TypeScript is widely used in front-end development, its adoption in back-end systems (especially with Node.js) is on the rise. This trend is likely to expand as frameworks like NestJS gain traction, enabling full- stack TypeScript development.

In conclusion, TypeScript has emerged as more than just an enhancement to JavaScript—it is shaping the future of web development itself. Its static typing, robust tooling, and increasing adoption across frameworks and libraries position TypeScript as an essential tool for any modern developer. As we move towards more complex, scalable applications in an ever-evolving tech landscape, embracing TypeScript becomes not just advantageous but necessary for those looking to build resilient, maintainable software.

TypeScript: Key Benefits and Features

In this chapter, we will explore the key benefits and features of TypeScript that contribute to its growing popularity among developers.

1. Strong Typing System

One of the most significant features of TypeScript is its optional static typing. This allows developers to define the types of variables, function parameters, and return values. With TypeScript, you can use interfaces and type annotations to specify and enforce types. This strong typing system offers numerous benefits:

Early Error Detection: TypeScript catches type-related errors at compile time instead of at runtime, significantly reducing potential bugs before deploying the code.

Improved Readability: Type definitions make code more self-documenting, making it easier for developers (including newcomers) to understand the intended use of various components.

Enhanced Tooling: Editors and IDEs gain the ability to provide more intelligent code completion, refactoring tools, and navigation assistance due to the explicit types.

2. Advanced Tooling and IDE Support

TypeScript has garnered robust support from various development environments and tools. Editors such as Visual Studio Code, Atom, and WebStorm take advantage of TypeScript's type system to offer:

Intelligent Code Completion: Autocomplete suggestions become more precise, with context-aware information, minimizing guesswork.

Real-Time Type Checking: Developers receive immediate feedback on type-related issues as they write code, fostering a more productive coding experience.

Refactoring Tools: TypeScript's understanding of code structures allows for advanced refactoring options, such as renaming variables or extracting methods seamlessly.

3. Enhanced JavaScript Features

TypeScript embraces the latest JavaScript features and often introduces additional ones, making it a feature- rich language. Developers can leverage:

Modern Syntax: TypeScript supports ES6 features such as arrow functions, async/await, destructuring, and more, ensuring that developers can utilize contemporary JavaScript syntax.

Decorators and Generics: These advanced constructs enable more flexible and reusable code design, allowing developers to create highly adaptable components.

4. Improved Code Maintenance

The scalability offered by TypeScript is particularly advantageous for larger codebases and teams:

Modular Architecture: TypeScript encourages modular programming through namespaces and modules, simplifying the organization of code into manageable chunks.

Documentation Generation: Tools like TypeDoc can generate documentation directly from TypeScript code, ensuring that documentation stays in sync with the actual implementation.

Better Collaboration: With type definitions and interfaces, team members can communicate expectations more clearly, reducing misunderstandings and facilitating collaboration.

5. Compatibility with Existing JavaScript

One of the most appealing aspects of TypeScript is its seamless integration with existing JavaScript codebases. You can gradually adopt TypeScript in a project without needing to rewrite everything from scratch. Key benefits include:

Interoperability: TypeScript can import existing JavaScript libraries and modules, allowing you to leverage existing code while gradually migrating to TypeScript.

Incremental Adoption: You can start using TypeScript in parts of an application and progressively migrate other parts over time, enabling a smoother transition.

6. Strong Community and Ecosystem

TypeScript has gained a robust community that contributes to a rich ecosystem. This includes:

Libraries and Frameworks: Major frameworks such as Angular, React, and Vue.js provide first-class support for TypeScript, offering type definitions out of the box and promoting best practices within the ecosystem.

Educational Resources: A wealth of tutorials, courses, and documentation is available for learning TypeScript, making it accessible for both beginners and seasoned developers alike.

By introducing a strong typing system, advanced tooling, enhanced JavaScript features, improved maintenance, and compatibility with existing code, TypeScript empowers developers to build scalable, maintainable, and error-resistant applications. As the development landscape continues to evolve, TypeScript stands out as a powerful tool that bridges the gap between flexibility and structure, ensuring that developers can harness the full potential of their code.

Chapter 2: Setting Up Your TypeScript Environment

In this chapter, we will walk through the steps needed to get your TypeScript environment up and running. By the end of this chapter, you will have a fully functional TypeScript setup that allows you to write, compile, and run TypeScript code with ease.

2.1 Prerequisites

Before diving into TypeScript, there are a few prerequisites you need to have in place. ### 2.1.1 Node.js

TypeScript is built on top of JavaScript, which means you'll need Node.js installed on your machine to run JavaScript and TypeScript programs. To check if you have Node.js installed, open your command line or terminal and run:

```bash
node -v
```

If Node.js is installed, you'll see a version number. If not, you can download the latest version from the [official Node.js website](https://nodejs.org/). Follow the installation instructions for your operating system.

2.1.2 Package Manager

Node.js typically comes with npm (Node Package Manager), which you will use to install TypeScript and other packages. To check if npm is installed, run:

```bash npm -v
```

If you see a version number, you're set to go. Otherwise, installing Node.js will also install npm. ## 2.2 Installing TypeScript

With Node.js and npm ready, it's time to install TypeScript. You can install TypeScript globally by running the following command in your terminal:

```bash
npm install -g typescript
```

The `-g` flag installs TypeScript globally, making it available across all your projects. To verify that TypeScript was installed successfully, run:

```bash tsc -v
```

This command will show the version of TypeScript that you've installed, confirming that the installation was successful.

2.3 Setting Up a Project Directory

Now that TypeScript is installed, it's wise to create a dedicated directory for your TypeScript projects. Create a new folder for your project and navigate into it. For example:

```bash
mkdir my-typescript-project cd my-typescript-project
```

```
```

Inside this folder, you can initialize a new npm project. This step is optional but highly recommended, as it helps manage your dependencies better:

```bash npm init -y
```

This command creates a `package.json` file with default values. This file is essential for managing your project dependencies and configurations.

2.4 Creating a TypeScript Configuration File

A TypeScript configuration file, usually named `tsconfig.json`, is essential for managing how your TypeScript code is compiled. You can create this file by executing:

```bash tsc --init
```

This command generates a default `tsconfig.json` file in your project directory. Let's take a moment to look at some of the key properties in this file:

compilerOptions: This section contains various options that control the behavior of the compiler, such as `target` (the version of JavaScript you want to compile to) and `module` (the module system you're using).

include: This property specifies which files or directories should be included for compilation.

exclude: Here you can list files or directories that should be excluded from the compilation process.

By default, the `tsconfig.json` file will have sensible defaults, but feel free to modify it according to your project requirements.

2.5 Writing Your First TypeScript File

With your environment set up, you're ready to write some TypeScript code! Create a new file called

`index.ts` in your project directory:

```bash
touch index.ts
```

Open `index.ts` in your favorite text editor and add the following code:

```typescript
function greet(name: string): string { return `Hello,
${name}!`;
}
console.log(greet("World"));
```

In this example, we define a simple function that takes a string as input and returns a greeting message. ## 2.6 Compiling TypeScript to JavaScript

To run your TypeScript code, you first need to compile it into JavaScript. You can do this by running:

```bash tsc
```

This command will compile all `.ts` files in the current directory according to the configurations defined in

`tsconfig.json`. After compiling, you should see a new file named `index.js` in your project directory. You can now run your compiled JavaScript file using Node.js:

```bash
node index.js
```

You should see the output: `Hello, World!` in your terminal. ## 2.7 Setting Up a Development Workflow

To streamline your development process, consider setting up a few tools:

2.7.1 File Watching

Instead of manually running the TypeScript compiler each time you change your code, you can use the `--watch` flag to automatically compile your TypeScript files when changes are detected:

```bash
tsc --watch
```

This command will continuously watch for changes in your `.ts` files and recompile them as needed. ### 2.7.2 Integrated Development Environments (IDEs)

Using an IDE can greatly enhance your TypeScript development experience. Popular choices include:

Visual Studio Code: A lightweight editor with excellent TypeScript support, including syntax highlighting, autocompletion, and debugging.

WebStorm: A powerful IDE from JetBrains that offers extensive support for TypeScript and other web development technologies.

By integrating TypeScript into an IDE, you can take advantage of features like error checking, code navigation, and version control support.

With your environment ready, you can now start exploring the rich features of TypeScript in your projects. In the next chapter, we'll delve deeper into the TypeScript language itself, exploring its types, interfaces, and more advanced features.

Installing TypeScript: Step-by-Step Guide

This guide will cover various installation methods, whether you're using Node.js, integrating with popular frameworks, or even working in a browser environment.

Prerequisites

Before we dive into the installation process, ensure that you have the following prerequisites:

Node.js and npm: TypeScript is typically installed via npm (Node Package Manager), which comes bundled with Node.js. Download and install Node.js from the official website: [Node.js](https://nodejs.org/). Follow the instructions for your operating system.

Text Editor or IDE: While you can technically write TypeScript in any text editor, having an IDE or editor with

TypeScript support will significantly enhance your development experience. Popular options include Visual Studio Code, IntelliJ IDEA, and WebStorm.

Command Line Interface: Familiarity with the command line is helpful since we'll be running some commands to install TypeScript.

Step 1: Check Node.js and npm Installation

After installing Node.js, verify that it is installed correctly by opening your terminal (Command Prompt on Windows or Terminal on macOS/Linux) and running the following commands:

```bash
node -v npm -v
```

These commands should output the versions of Node.js and npm installed on your system. If you see the version numbers, congratulations, you have successfully installed Node.js and npm!

Step 2: Installing TypeScript Globally

To use TypeScript in any project or from any directory, you can install it globally. This is the most common approach for developers who are starting with TypeScript. Run the following command in your terminal:

```bash
npm install -g typescript
```

The `-g` flag indicates a global installation. This command may require administrative privileges depending on your operating system.

Verification of Global Installation

Once the installation is complete, you can verify that TypeScript is installed by checking its version:

```bash
tsc -v
```

The output should display the current version of TypeScript, confirming that the installation was successful. ## Step 3: Setting Up a TypeScript Project

With TypeScript installed, let's create a new project and configure it. Here's how to do it step-by-step: ### Step 3.1: Create a New Directory

Open your terminal and create a new directory for your TypeScript project:

```bash
mkdir my-typescript-project cd my-typescript-project
```

Step 3.2: Initialize a Package.json File

To help manage your dependencies, it's a good practice to create a `package.json` file. You can do this by running:

```bash
npm init -y
```

This command creates a basic `package.json` file with default settings. ### Step 3.3: Install TypeScript Locally

In addition to global installation, you may want to install TypeScript locally for your project. This can help manage dependencies specific to the project without affecting others. Run:

```bash
npm install typescript --save-dev
```

The `--save-dev` flag adds TypeScript to your project's development dependencies. ### Step 3.4: Initialize a TypeScript Configuration File

A TypeScript configuration file, `tsconfig.json`, is essential for defining the compiler options and the structure of your TypeScript project. You can create a basic configuration file by running:

```bash
npx tsc --init
```

This command generates a `tsconfig.json` file with sensible default settings. You can modify this file later to customize your TypeScript compilation settings.

Step 4: Writing Your First TypeScript File

Now that TypeScript is installed and your project is set up, let's create a simple TypeScript file to ensure everything is working. Create a new file named `index.ts`:

```bash
touch index.ts
```

Open `index.ts` in your text editor, and add the following

code:

```typescript
let message: string = "Hello, TypeScript!";
console.log(message);
```

Step 5: Compiling TypeScript

To compile your TypeScript code to JavaScript, you will use the TypeScript compiler. Run the following command in your terminal:

```bash
npx tsc
```

This command compiles all TypeScript files in the project (in this case, `index.ts`) into JavaScript. You should see a new file named `index.js` in your project directory.

Step 5.1: Running Your Compiled Code

Now you can run the compiled JavaScript code using Node.js:

```bash
node index.js
```

You should see the output: `"Hello, TypeScript!"`, confirming that your installation and setup are successful.

You've successfully installed TypeScript and set up your first project. You now have a basic understanding of how to create, compile, and run TypeScript code.

Configuring tsconfig.json for Your Project

In this chapter, we will delve into the purpose of `tsconfig.json`, explore its key properties, and provide practical examples to ensure your TypeScript project is set up correctly.

What is tsconfig.json?

The `tsconfig.json` file is a JSON configuration file that specifies the compiler options required to compile a TypeScript project. It can define settings that affect how TypeScript code is compiled, as well as which files are included in the compilation process. It's essentially the brain of your TypeScript project, guiding the compiler on how to interpret your code.

Benefits of `tsconfig.json`

Type Safety and Error Checking: By configuring strict type-checking options, you can catch errors at compile time rather than at runtime.

File Inclusion and Exclusion: Control which files the compiler should include or exclude from the build process.

Compiler Options: Tailor the output of your compiled JavaScript to meet specific needs (e.g., targeting different ECMAScript versions).

Development Workflow: Enhance your development workflow with options for source maps, declaration files, and other settings that improve the development experience.

31

Creating a tsconfig.json File

To create a `tsconfig.json` file, navigate to your project directory in the terminal and run the following command:

```bash
tsc --init
```

This command initializes a `tsconfig.json` file with default settings, which you can then customize according to your project's requirements.

Key Properties of tsconfig.json

The `tsconfig.json` file consists of several key properties that determine how the TypeScript compiler behaves. Let's explore some of the most commonly used properties:

1. `compilerOptions`

The `compilerOptions` object allows you to specify various compiler settings. Here are some crucial options:

- **`target`**: Specifies the ECMAScript version to which you want to compile your TypeScript code. Common values include `"ES5"`, `"ES6"` (or `"ES2015"`), and `"ESNext"`.

```json
"compilerOptions": { "target": "ES6"
}
```

- **`module`**: Defines the module system used in your project. Options include `"CommonJS"`, `"ES6"`, `"AMD"`, among others.

```json
"compilerOptions": { "module": "CommonJS"
```

```
}
```

- **`strict`**: Enables all strict type-checking options at once, which is highly recommended for improving type safety:

```json "compilerOptions": { "strict": true
```

```
}
```

- **`sourceMap`**: Generates corresponding `.map` files for your TypeScript files, which can be useful for debugging.

```json "compilerOptions": { "sourceMap": true
```

```
}
```

- **`outDir`**: Specifies the output directory for the compiled JavaScript files.

```json "compilerOptions": { "outDir": "./dist"
```

```
}
```

- **`rootDir`**: Specifies the root directory of input files. This helps maintain a clean project structure.

```json "compilerOptions": { "rootDir": "./src"
```

```
}
```

2. `include` and `exclude`

These properties allow you to control which files are included or excluded in the compilation process. The

`include` property specifies an array of file paths or glob patterns to include, while the `exclude` property specifies an array of paths to exclude.

```json
{
"include": ["src/**/*"],

"exclude": ["node_modules", "**/*.spec.ts"]
}
```

3. `extends`

If you want to extend a base configuration file, you can use the `extends` property. This is particularly useful for sharing common configurations across multiple projects.

```json
{
"extends": "./base-tsconfig.json"
}
```

4. `paths` and `baseUrl`

The `paths` and `baseUrl` options help you manage module resolution. They allow you to define base paths for module lookups and create path aliases for easier imports.

```json
"compilerOptions": { "baseUrl": "./src", "paths": {
  "@components/*": ["components/*"]
}
}
```

Customizing Your tsconfig.json

Now that you are familiar with the key properties of `tsconfig.json`, here is an example configuration that incorporates several options to create a robust TypeScript project setup:

```json
{
"compilerOptions": { "target": "ES2020", "module": "CommonJS", "strict": true, "esModuleInterop": true,
"forceConsistentCasingInFileNames": true, "outDir": "./dist",
"rootDir": "./src", "sourceMap": true
},
"include": ["src/**/*"],
"exclude": ["node_modules", "**/*.spec.ts"]
}
```

This configuration targets ECMAScript 2020, uses CommonJS modules, and enables strict type checking while generating source maps and controlling file organization through `outDir` and `rootDir`.

By customizing compiler options, defining file inclusions, and controlling module resolution, you can create a more efficient and error-free development environment.

Chapter 3: TypeScript Basics

In this chapter, we will delve into the fundamental concepts and features of TypeScript that make it a preferred choice for modern web development.

3.1 What is TypeScript?

TypeScript is an open-source programming language developed by Microsoft. It builds upon JavaScript by adding optional static typing and other features such as interfaces, enums, and access modifiers. The most significant advantage of TypeScript is that it allows developers to write cleaner and more maintainable code. Furthermore, TypeScript code compiles down to plain JavaScript, which means it can be executed anywhere JavaScript runs.

3.1.1 Key Features of TypeScript

Static Typing: TypeScript allows developers to define types explicitly, which helps prevent common errors during compilation.

Enhanced Code Editor Support: Many modern IDEs offer rich support for TypeScript, providing features such as auto-completion, type checking, and refactoring tools.

Interfaces: TypeScript introduces the concept of interfaces, which help define contracts for classes and objects.

Namespaces and Modules: TypeScript supports the organization of code through namespaces and modules, promoting better structure and code encapsulation.

Decorators: TypeScript allows the use of decorators, which enable the modification of classes and methods at runtime.

3.2 Setting Up TypeScript

To begin working with TypeScript, you'll first need to install it. You can easily add TypeScript to your project using npm:

```bash
npm install -g typescript
```

After installing TypeScript globally, you can check the installed version with:

```bash tsc -v
```

Once you have TypeScript installed, you can create a new TypeScript file with the `.ts` extension. For example, let's create a file called `app.ts`.

3.3 Basic Types

TypeScript provides several built-in types, which can be used to define the type of variables, function parameters, and return values. Here are some of the basic types:

Number: Represents both integer and floating-point numbers.

```typescript
let age: number = 25;
```

String: Represents a sequence of characters.

```typescript
```

```typescript
let name: string = "Alice";
```

Boolean: Represents a true/false value.

```typescript
let isActive: boolean = true;
```

Array: Represents a collection of values.

```typescript
let scores: number[] = [90, 80, 85];
```

Tuple: Represents an array with fixed types.

```typescript
let user: [string, number] = ["Alice", 25];
```

Any: Represents any type, which can be very flexible but can also be risky if overused.

```typescript
let randomValue: any = 42; randomValue = "Hello";
```

3.4 Type Annotations

Type annotations help developers specify the type for a variable or function parameters. This is how you can use type annotations with the variables we discussed earlier:

```typescript
```

```
let username: string; let quantity: number;
let isAvailable: boolean;
```
```

Type annotations can also be applied to function
arguments and return types. Here's an example:

```typescript
function greet(name: string): string { return `Hello,
${name}`;
}
```

In the above function, `name` is of type `string`, and the
function returns a string as well.

3.5 Interfaces in TypeScript

Interfaces are a way to define custom types in TypeScript.
They allow for the creation of reusable class contracts,
ensuring that certain properties or methods are available.

Here's a simple example of an interface:

```typescript interface Person {

name: string; age: number; greet(): string;
}

const person: Person = { name: "Alice",

age: 30, greet() {

return `Hello, my name is ${this.name} and I'm
${this.age} years old.`;
}
```
```

```
};
```

In the example above, we define a `Person` interface with three members: `name`, `age`, and the method

`greet`. The object `person` implements this interface. ## 3.6 Classes and Inheritance

TypeScript enhances JavaScript's class-based syntax with additional features, such as constructors and access modifiers (public, private, protected). Here is an example of a class with inheritance:

```typescript
class Animal {

constructor(public name: string) {}

speak(): string {

return `${this.name} makes a noise.`;

}

}

class Dog extends Animal { speak(): string {

return `${this.name} barks.`;

}

}

const dog = new Dog("Rex"); console.log(dog.speak()); // Output: Rex barks.
```

In this chapter, we covered the basics of TypeScript, including its key features, how to set it up, and fundamental concepts like types, type annotations, interfaces, and classes. By leveraging these features, developers can create robust and scalable applications with greater ease.

Variables and Data Types in TypeScript

One of the core concepts in any programming language is its approach to variables and data types. Understanding how to declare variables and use data types in TypeScript is fundamental to writing effective and efficient TypeScript code. In this chapter, we will delve deep into the various types of variables, their declarations, and the rich set of data types that TypeScript offers.

1. Understanding Variables

In programming, a variable is a container for holding data values. In TypeScript, like in JavaScript, you can declare variables using the `let`, `const`, or `var` keywords. The choice of which keyword to use can influence the variable's scope and mutability.

1.1 Variable Declaration

let: This keyword is used for declaring variables that can be reassigned later. It has block scope, meaning it is only accessible within the block it is defined.

```typescript
let count = 10;

count = 20; // This is valid
```

const: This keyword is used for declaring variables that are constant and cannot be reassigned after their initial assignment. Like `let`, `const` also has block scope.

```typescript
const pi = 3.14;
// pi = 3.14159; // This would throw an error
```

var: This keyword is function-scoped or globally-scoped (if declared outside a function) and is generally less common in modern TypeScript (and JavaScript) code due to its quirks and potential for introducing bugs.

```typescript
var message = "Hello, World!"; message = "Hello, Universe!";
```

1.2 Scope of Variables

Understanding the scope of variables is crucial for avoiding errors and optimizing code performance. Variables declared with `let` and `const` are block-scoped, whereas variables declared using `var` are function-scoped. This means that a variable declared inside a block (like an `if` statement or a loop) with

`let` or `const` will not be accessible outside that block.

```typescript
if (true) {
let blockVar = "I am block scoped!"; console.log(blockVar); // This will work
}
console.log(blockVar); // This will throw an error
```

2. Data Types in TypeScript

TypeScript introduces a rich set of data types to help developers define their variables more explicitly, aiding in both documentation and error-checking. Understanding these data types is essential for effective TypeScript programming.

2.1 Basic Data Types

TypeScript provides several basic data types, each serving a different purpose:

Number: Represents numeric values, both integer and floating-point.

```typescript
let age: number = 25;

let temperature: number = 18.5;
```

String: Represents textual data enclosed in single or double quotes.

```typescript
let name: string = "Alice";
```

Boolean: Represents a logical value, either `true` or `false`.

```typescript
let isActive: boolean = true;
```

2.2 Special Data Types

Beyond basic types, TypeScript offers a variety of special data types:

Any: This type allows for any kind of value to be assigned. It is generally discouraged unless necessary, as it bypasses TypeScript's type-checking.

```typescript
let randomValue: any = 10; randomValue = "Could be a string now";
```

Unknown: Similar to `any`, but safer. You can't perform operations on an `unknown` type until you assert it to a specific type.

```typescript
let userInput: unknown;

userInput = "This could be anything";
```

Void: Used to indicate that a function does not return a value.

```typescript
function logMessage(message: string): void {
console.log(message);

}
```

Null and Undefined: Represents intentional absence of any value.

```typescript
let notAssigned: null = null;
let uninitialized: undefined = undefined;
```

2.3 Arrays and Tuples

TypeScript allows developers to create arrays and tuples, which are collections of values that can hold multiple entries.

Arrays: Can contain multiple values of the same type.

```typescript
let numbers: number[] = [1, 2, 3, 4, 5];
let names: string[] = ["Alice", "Bob", "Charlie"];
```

Tuples: Can contain a fixed amount of values of different types.

```typescript
let tuple: [string, number] = ["Alice", 30];
```

2.4 Enumerations

Enumerations, or enums, allow for defining a set of named constants. This improves the readability of code by replacing numeric values with descriptive names.

```typescript enum Color{ Red,
Green, Blue,
}
```

```
let myColor: Color = Color.Red;
```
` ` `

Understanding variables and data types is a crucial step towards becoming proficient in TypeScript. The choice of variable declaration keywords and the rich set of data types provided by TypeScript helps developers write safer, clearer, and more maintainable code.

Type Annotations and Type Inference

This empowers developers to write safer, more predictable code. In this chapter, we will explore two key features of TypeScript: type annotations and type inference. We'll delve into how they work, their benefits, and practical examples to illustrate their use.

Understanding Type Annotations

Type annotations in TypeScript are explicit declarations made by developers to specify the type of a variable, function parameter, or return value. By providing these annotations, developers communicate their intentions to both the compiler and other programmers. This process contributes to better documentation, easier debugging, and enhanced code quality.

Basic Type Annotations

Type annotations are straightforward and can be applied to various types, including primitives, arrays, objects, and more complex data structures. The syntax for a type annotation is simple:

```typescript
let variableName: Type = value;
```

Example:

```typescript
let age: number = 30;
let name: string = "Alice"; let isActive: boolean = true;
```

In this example, `age`, `name`, and `isActive` have been given type annotations, indicating they should hold a number, a string, and a boolean, respectively. If you try to assign a value of a different type, TypeScript will throw a compile-time error, promoting type safety.

Function Parameter and Return Type Annotations

Type annotations not only apply to variables but also to function parameters and return types. This allows you to define what types of arguments a function can accept and what type it will return.

Example:

```typescript
function greet(person: string): string { return `Hello, ${person}!`;
}
let greeting: string = greet("Bob");
```

In the `greet` function, the `person` parameter is typed

as `string`, and the function itself is defined to return a string. Attempting to pass a different type will raise an error:

```typescript
greet(42); // Error: Argument of type 'number' is not assignable to parameter of type 'string'.
```

Exploring Type Inference

Type inference is one of TypeScript's most powerful features. It enables the compiler to automatically deduce the type of a variable based on its initialization value. This means that type annotations are not always necessary, as TypeScript can infer types from the context.

Automatic Type Inference

When a variable is initialized with a specific value, TypeScript automatically assigns the relevant type to that variable.

Example:

```typescript
let score = 100; // TypeScript infers the type as number

let message = "Welcome!"; // TypeScript infers the type as string let isLoggedIn = false; // TypeScript infers the type as boolean
```

In this example, even though we didn't specify the types explicitly, TypeScript correctly infers them based on the values assigned to each variable.

Contextual Typing

TypeScript goes a step further with contextual typing, which is particularly useful in the context of functions and callbacks. When a function is assigned to a variable, TypeScript can infer the types based on the expected structure of the function.

Example:

```typescript
let numbers = [1, 2, 3];

let doubledNumbers = numbers.map(n => n * 2); // TypeScript infers 'n' as number
```

In this example, the arrow function parameter `n` is inferred to be a number because of its use within the

`map` method applied to the `numbers` array. ### Limitations of Type Inference

While type inference is powerful, it is not foolproof. Some complex scenarios may lead to less accurate type inference, prompting the need for explicit type annotations. Understanding when to provide these annotations can greatly enhance code clarity and maintainability.

Example of Limitations:

```typescript
let value; // TypeScript infers 'any'

value = 15; // value type is inferred as number
```

```
value = "Hello"; // still allowed because 'value' is type 'any'
```
```

In the above code, the implicit `any` type of `value` allows any kind of assignment. This can lead to bugs that are hard to trace. To mitigate this, explicitly declaring the type can enforce stricter safety:

```typescript
let value: number; // Now value can only be a number
```

By using type annotations, you can clarify your intent and prevent errors, while type inference allows for cleaner code without verbosity.
```

Chapter 4: Working with Functions in TypeScript

In this chapter, we will explore how to create functions in TypeScript, understand their types and signatures, delve into function overloads, and discuss some advanced concepts related to functions.

4.1 Defining Functions

In TypeScript, you can define functions in several ways: function declarations, function expressions, and arrow functions. Let's look at each style of defining functions.

4.1.1 Function Declarations

A function declaration defines a named function. The basic syntax is as follows:

```typescript
function functionName(parameter1: type1, parameter2: type2): returnType {
// Function body
}
```

Example:

```typescript
function add(a: number, b: number): number { return a + b;
}
const result = add(5, 10); // result is 15
```

```
```

In this example, the `add` function takes two parameters `a` and `b`, both of which are of type `number`, and returns a value of type `number`.

4.1.2 Function Expressions

You can also define a function as a part of an expression. This is commonly used for anonymous functions or when assigning functions to variables.

Example:

```typescript
const multiply = function (a: number, b: number): number
{ return a * b;
};
const product = multiply(5, 10); // product is 50
```

4.1.3 Arrow Functions

Arrow functions are a more concise way to write function expressions and are often preferred for their simplicity and lexically scoped `this`.

Example:

```typescript
const divide = (a: number, b: number): number => {
return a / b;
};
const quotient = divide(10, 2); // quotient is 5
```

4.1.4 Optional and Default Parameters

TypeScript allows you to define optional parameters using the question mark (`?`) and default parameters with an equals sign (`=`).

Example:

```typescript
function greet(name: string, greeting: string = "Hello"): string { return `${greeting}, ${name}!`;
}
console.log(greet("John")); // Outputs: "Hello, John!"
console.log(greet("John", "Good morning")); // Outputs: "Good morning, John!"
```

4.2 Function Types

Functions in TypeScript are first-class citizens, which means you can also define types for function signatures. The syntax for defining a function type is:

```typescript
type FunctionType = (parameter1: type1, parameter2: type2) => returnType;
```

Example:

```typescript
type MathOperation = (x: number, y: number) => number; const subtract: MathOperation = (x, y) => x - y;
console.log(subtract(10, 5)); // Outputs: 5
```

```
```

4.3 Function Overloading

TypeScript allows function overloading, whereby you can define multiple signatures for a function based on different parameter types. The implementation, however, must be a single function.

Example:

```typescript
function combine(input1: number, input2: number): number; function combine(input1: string, input2: string): string; function combine(input1: any, input2: any): any {
return input1 + input2;

}
console.log(combine(5, 10)); // Outputs: 15
console.log(combine("Hello, ", "world!")); // Outputs: "Hello, world!"
```

In this example, the `combine` function can take either two numbers or two strings and return the result accordingly.

4.4 Rest Parameters

The rest parameters feature allows you to represent an indefinite number of arguments as an array. This can be useful when you do not know the exact number of parameters beforehand.

Example:

```typescript
```

```typescript
function sum(...numbers: number[]): number {
return numbers.reduce((acc, num) => acc + num, 0);
}
console.log(sum(1, 2, 3, 4, 5)); // Outputs: 15
```

4.5 Callbacks and Higher-Order Functions

Functions in TypeScript can also accept other functions as arguments or return them as results. This allows for powerful programming paradigms such as callbacks and higher-order functions.

Example:

```typescript
function processNumbers(numbers: number[], action: (num: number) => void): void { for (const num of numbers) {
action(num);
}
}
processNumbers([1, 2, 3], (num) => {
console.log(num * 2); // Outputs: 2, 4, 6
});
```

4.5.1 Returning Functions

TypeScript also supports returning functions from other functions, enabling closures and factory functions.

Example:

```typescript
function makeMultiplier(factor: number): (num: number)
=> number { return function(num: number): number {

return num * factor;

};

}

const double = makeMultiplier(2); console.log(double(5));
// Outputs: 10
```

Understanding these aspects will enable you to write more robust, type-safe, and maintainable code in TypeScript.

Function Parameters and Return Types

This feature allows developers to catch errors during the development phase rather than at runtime, creating a more robust and maintainable codebase. One of the core elements of TypeScript's type system is the ability to define function parameters and return types explicitly.

In this chapter, we will explore how to declare function parameters and their types, specify return types for functions, and understand the importance of these features in improving code quality and readability. We will also discuss default parameters, optional parameters, and the use of rest parameters to handle a variable number of arguments.

Function Parameters

In TypeScript, you can define types for the parameters of functions to ensure that the values passed in during the function call conform to expected types. This helps prevent type-related errors and makes the code easier to follow and maintain.

Basic Parameter Types

Here's a simple example of a function with typed parameters:

```typescript
function greet(name: string): void { console.log(`Hello, ${name}!`);
}
greet("Alice");
// Outputs: Hello, Alice!
```

In this example, the `greet` function expects a single parameter called `name`, which is of type `string`. The return type of this function is `void`, indicating that it does not return any value.

Multiple Parameters

Functions can accept multiple parameters, each of which can have its own type:

```typescript
function add(a: number, b: number): number { return a + b;
```

```
}
```

const sum = add(5, 10); console.log(sum); // Outputs: 15

```
` ` `
```

In the `add` function, both `a` and `b` are specified as `number` types, and the function is expected to return a `number`.

Default Parameters

TypeScript allows you to define default values for function parameters. If an argument is not provided, the default value is used:

```typescript
function multiply(a: number, b: number = 1): number {
return a * b;
}
console.log(multiply(5));        //        Outputs:        5
console.log(multiply(5, 2)); // Outputs: 10
` ` `
```

In this example, `b` has a default value of `1`. If the caller does not provide a second argument, `b` will default to `1`.

Optional Parameters

You can also make parameters optional by appending a question mark (`?`) to the parameter name. If the caller does not provide an argument for an optional parameter, it is treated as `undefined`:

```typescript
function log(message: string, userId?: number): void {
console.log(`Message: ${message}`);

if (userId !== undefined) { console.log(`User ID: ${userId}`);
}

}

log("User logged in");      // Outputs: Message: User logged in log("User logged out", 42); // Outputs: Message: User logged out

// User ID: 42
```

Here, `userId` is optional. If it isn't provided, the `log` function still runs without any errors, and it can handle the absence of `userId` gracefully.

Rest Parameters

Sometimes, you might want to handle a variable number of arguments. In that case, you can use rest parameters, indicated by `...` followed by the parameter name. This allows you to capture multiple arguments as an array:

```typescript
function sumAll(...numbers: number[]): number { return numbers.reduce((acc, cur) => acc + cur, 0);
}

console.log(sumAll(1, 2, 3, 4, 5)); // Outputs: 15
```

In this `sumAll` function, `numbers` is an array of `number` types, and you can pass any number of numeric arguments.

Return Types

Specifying a return type for a function is crucial in TypeScript. By defining the expected return type, you provide clear documentation about what a caller can expect, which enhances maintainability and reduces the risk of errors.

Explicit Return Type

You can explicitly specify the return type of a function:

```typescript
function divide(a: number, b: number): number { return a / b;
}
const result = divide(10, 2); console.log(result); // Outputs: 5
```

In this example, the return type of the `divide` function is specified as `number`. ### Implicit Return Types

Often, TypeScript can infer the return type based on the function's implementation:

```typescript
function square(x: number) {

return x * x; // TypeScript infers this as number
```

```
}
const            squareResult         =              square(3);
console.log(squareResult); // Outputs: 9
```

While implicit return types can be convenient, explicitly stating return types is beneficial for clarity. ### Handling Different Return Types

You may encounter scenarios where a function could return different types. TypeScript allows you to use union types to specify this:

```typescript
function getValue(key: string): number | undefined { const values: { [key: string]: number } = {

"a": 1,

"b": 2,

};

return values[key]; // could return a number or undefined

}

const valueA = getValue("a"); // number const valueB = getValue("b"); // number const valueC = getValue("c"); // undefined
```

In this `getValue` function, the return type is `number | undefined`, indicating that the function can return a number or `undefined` if the key does not exist.

Understanding and effectively using function parameters

and return types in TypeScript is essential for creating reliable and maintainable code. By leveraging TypeScript's type system, developers can ensure that functions are called with the correct types and that they return the expected values, significantly reducing the risk of errors.

Arrow Functions, Optional & Default Parameters

In this chapter, we'll delve into each of these features, demonstrating how they work, why they are useful, and how they can improve your programming experience in TypeScript.

1. Arrow Functions

Arrow functions are a syntactically compact alternative to traditional function expressions in JavaScript and TypeScript. They are particularly useful for preserving the lexical scope of the `this` keyword, making them invaluable in many programming scenarios, especially while working with classes or in callback functions.

1.1 Syntax of Arrow Functions

The basic syntax of an arrow function is as follows:

```typescript
const functionName = (parameters) => {
// Function body
};
```

1.2 Example of Arrow Functions

Consider a simple example where we have a regular function and its arrow function equivalent:

```typescript
function add(x: number, y: number): number { return x +
y;
}

const addArrow = (x: number, y: number): number => {
return x + y;
};

// Usage
console.log(add(5, 10));    // Output: 15
console.log(addArrow(5, 10)); // Output: 15
```

In this example, both functions perform the same operation, but the arrow function syntax is more concise.

1.3 Lexical `this`

One of the most notable features of arrow functions is their handling of the `this` keyword. In traditional functions, `this` is determined by how a function is called. However, in arrow functions, `this` is lexically inherited from the outer scope.

```typescript
class Counter {

count: number = 0;

increment() { setTimeout(function() {

this.count++; // 'this' refers to the global object or
undefined in strict mode console.log(this.count);
```

```
}, 1000);
}
incrementArrow() { setTimeout(() => {
this.count++; // 'this' refers to the instance of Counter
console.log(this.count);
}, 1000);
}
}
const counter = new Counter();
counter.increment();        // Output: NaN after 1 second
counter.incrementArrow(); // Output: 1 after 1 second
```

In the above code, the `increment` method with a traditional function fails to access the class instance's

`this`, whereas `incrementArrow` correctly accesses it.
1.4 Conclusion on Arrow Functions

Arrow functions allow developers to write more concise and readable code while avoiding common pitfalls associated with the `this` keyword. They are an essential feature to adopt in TypeScript to enhance code maintainability.

2. Optional Parameters

Optional parameters in TypeScript allow developers to specify whether an argument is required or not. This is particularly useful when you want to provide flexibility in function calls while maintaining type safety.

2.1 Syntax of Optional Parameters

Optional parameters are defined by appending a question mark (`?`) to the parameter name in the function declaration.

```typescript
function greet(name: string, age?: number): string { if (age) {

return `Hello, ${name}. You are ${age} years old.`;

}

return `Hello, ${name}.`;

}
```

2.2 Example of Optional Parameters

Using the `greet` function, we can call it with one or both parameters:

```typescript
console.log(greet("Alice")); // Output: Hello, Alice.


console.log(greet("Bob", 30));     // Output: Hello, Bob. You are 30 years old.
```

In this example, the `age` parameter is optional. If it isn't provided, the function will execute without any issues.

2.3 Benefits of Optional Parameters

Flexibility: Functions can accept a varying number of

66

arguments without throwing errors.

Type Safety: TypeScript still provides type checking, ensuring that if parameters are provided, they adhere to the specified types.

3. Default Parameters

Default parameters allow you to set default values for function parameters, providing a fallback value when none is supplied.

3.1 Syntax of Default Parameters

To declare a default parameter, simply assign a value to it in the function declaration:

```typescript
function multiply(x: number, y: number = 2): number {
return x * y;

}
```

3.2 Example of Default Parameters

Using the `multiply` function, we see how it operates with and without the second argument:

```typescript
console.log(multiply(5));   // Output: 10 (5 * 2)

console.log(multiply(5, 3));// Output: 15 (5 * 3)
```

3.3 Key Advantages of Default Parameters

Reduced Overloading: Default parameters can eliminate the need for multiple overloaded function signatures.

Code Clarity: Default parameters can make it clear what the typical usage of a function is.

By mastering these features, developers can create robust, maintainable, and type-safe applications, leveraging TypeScript's full potential. In practice, using these features together can lead to cleaner and more efficient code, which is a fundamental goal for any developer striving for excellence in software development.

Chapter 5: Understanding Interfaces and Types

In this chapter, we will delve into the concepts of interfaces and types in TypeScript, explore their differences and similarities, and provide practical examples to illustrate their usage.

5.1 What are Interfaces?

In TypeScript, an interface is a syntactical contract that an entity should conform to. It defines the shape of an object, specifying what properties and methods an object should possess. Interfaces can be used to describe objects, functions, or arrays, making them a versatile feature in TypeScript.

Declaring an Interface

To declare an interface, we use the `interface` keyword followed by the name of the interface and its properties:

```typescript
interface User {
id: number; name: string; email: string;
isActive?: boolean; // Optional property
}
```

In this example, the `User` interface describes an object that should have an `id`, `name`, `email`, and an optional `isActive` property.

Implementing an Interface

Classes can implement interfaces to ensure they adhere to the defined structure:

```typescript
class UserAccount implements User {
constructor(public id: number, public name: string, public email: string, public isActive: boolean = true) {}

displayUser() {
console.log(`User: ${this.name}, Email: ${this.email}`);
}
}
```

The `UserAccount` class implements the `User` interface and provides a method to display user information. This guarantees that any instance of `UserAccount` will conform to the `User` interface.

5.2 What are Types?

In TypeScript, a type can be viewed as a synonym for a data structure. While interfaces are primarily used for object shapes, types can cover a wider range of scenarios. They can represent primitive types, unions, intersections, tuples, and even more complex structures.

Declaring a Type

Types are declared using the `type` keyword, and they offer flexibility that interfaces may not.

```typescript
type StringOrNumber = string | number;
let value: StringOrNumber; value = 42; // Valid
```

value = "TypeScript"; // Valid
```

In the example above, `StringOrNumber` is a union type that can either be a string or a number. #### Using Types for Objects

Types can also define the shape of objects, similar to interfaces:

```typescript type Product = {

id: number; name: string; price: number;

tags?: string[]; // Optional property

};

const product: Product = { id: 1,

name: "Laptop", price: 999.99,

};
```

5.3 Interfaces vs. Types

It is essential to understand the differences and when to use interfaces versus types:

Declaration Merging: Interfaces can be merged. You can declare the same interface multiple times, and TypeScript will combine them:

```typescript interface Vehicle {

make: string;

}

interface Vehicle { model: string;

```
}
const car: Vehicle = { make: "Toyota", model: "Camry"
};
```
` ` `

In contrast, types cannot be declared multiple times.

**Extensibility**: Interfaces can extend other interfaces using the `extends` keyword:

```typescript interface Animal {
name: string;
}
interface Dog extends Animal { breed: string;
}
```
` ` `

While types can achieve similar functionality using intersections (e.g., `type Dog = Animal & { breed: string; }`), the syntax is slightly different.

Use Cases: Interfaces are typically preferred when defining the shapes of objects or class contracts, while types are more fitting for utility types, unions, or when working with other complex types.

5.4 Practical Examples

Example 1: Using Interfaces for Function Types
Interfaces can also define function types:

```typescript
interface UserCallback { (user: User): void;
```

```
}
const    logUser:    UserCallback    =    (user)    =>    {
console.log(`${user.name} has the email ${user.email}`);
};
```
` ` `

In this example, `UserCallback` defines a function type that takes a `User` object and returns `void`. #### Example 2: Using Types for Complex Structures

Types can allow for more complex constructs. Here's an example using a tuple type:

` ` `typescript

```
type Response = [number, string];

const apiResponse: Response = [200, "Success"];
```
` ` `

In this case, `Response` is defined as a tuple consisting of a number and a string, providing a simple structure for an API response.

By using interfaces for contracts and types for flexibility, developers can create robustly typed applications that are easy to maintain. As you continue to work with TypeScript, you will find that mastering interfaces and types will greatly enhance your development experience.

Using Interfaces for Object Structures

In this chapter, we will explore how to use interfaces for defining object structures in TypeScript, with real- world examples to solidify understanding.

What is an Interface?

An interface in TypeScript is a syntactical contract that a class or an object can follow. It defines a structure that dictates what properties and methods an object can have. Interfaces do not produce any JavaScript output; instead, they serve as a compile-time check for ensuring that the objects adhere to the defined shape.

Defining an Interface

To define an interface in TypeScript, we use the `interface` keyword followed by the name of the interface. Here's a straightforward example:

```typescript
interface User {
id: number; name: string; email: string;
}
```

In this example, we've defined a `User` interface that mandates any user object to have an `id`, `name`, and

`email`. Each property must conform to the specified type, ensuring consistency across your application. ## Implementing Interfaces

Once an interface is defined, you can create objects that implement it. This can be done directly or through classes. Here's how you can create an object that adheres to the `User` interface:

```typescript
const user: User = { id: 1,
name: 'Alice',
```

74

```typescript
email: 'alice@example.com'
};
```

Using Interfaces with Classes

Interfaces can be used with classes to enforce structure. Here's how:

```typescript
class Admin implements User { id: number;

name: string; email: string; role: string;

constructor(id: number, name: string, email: string, role: string) { this.id = id; this.name = name; this.email = email; this.role = role;

}
}
```

In this example, the `Admin` class implements the `User` interface, ensuring that all properties defined in the interface are present in the class. Furthermore, we added an additional property, `role`, specific to the

`Admin` class.

Optional Properties

TypeScript allows you to define optional properties in an interface. By adding a question mark (`?`) after the property name, you indicate that it may or may not exist.

```typescript interface User {

id: number; name: string; email: string;
```

```typescript
phoneNumber?: string; // optional property
}
```

In this scenario, a `User` can choose to provide a `phoneNumber`, but it is not mandatory. This feature enables flexibility when dealing with complex object structures.

Readonly Properties

Another aspect of interfaces is the ability to define properties as `readonly`. This makes them immutable after the object has been created:

```typescript
interface User {
readonly id: number; name: string;
email: string;
}
```

With `readonly` properties, the `id` of the `User` cannot change after the initial assignment, thus protecting the integrity of the data.

Extending Interfaces

TypeScript supports the concept of extending interfaces, allowing for more complex hierarchies and structures. You can create a new interface based on an existing one using the `extends` keyword:

```typescript
interface Admin extends User { permissions: string[];
```

```
}
```

Here, the `Admin` interface inherits the properties of the `User` interface and adds a new property,

`permissions`, which is an array of strings. This is particularly useful when you want to build upon existing structures without duplicating code.

Function Types

Interfaces in TypeScript can also define function types, adding even more versatility to your object structures. Here's an example:

```typescript
interface User {

id: number; name: string; email: string;

greet: (greeting: string) => string; // defining a method within the interface

}
```

In this case, the `User` interface requires a `greet` method that takes a string parameter and returns a string. You can implement this interface as shown below:

```typescript
const user: User = { id: 1,

name: 'Bob',

email: 'bob@example.com', greet(greeting: string): string {

return `${greeting}, my name is ${this.name}.`;

}
```

```
};
```

console.log(user.greet("Hello")); // Output: Hello, my name is Bob.
```
```
```

By leveraging interfaces, developers can enforce consistency across codebases, enhancing maintainability and reducing the chances of runtime errors. The flexibility of optional properties, readonly fields, and function types allows for detailed and expressive design, making TypeScript an invaluable tool for modern web development.

# Differences Between Types and Interfaces

While they share some similarities and can often be used interchangeably, there are key differences that every developer should understand to harness the full power of TypeScript effectively.

## 1. Definitions and Basic Syntax ### What are Types?

In TypeScript, a **type** can represent a variety of types, including primitive types, union types, intersection types, and more. The type keyword is used to define an alias for any type. Here's a simple example of defining a type:

```typescript
type User = {
```

name: string; age: number; email: string;
```
};
```
```
```
```

What are Interfaces?

An **interface** is primarily used to define the structure of an object, detailing the properties and their types. Interfaces are more geared towards objects and are heavily used in object-oriented programming. Here's how you define an interface:

```typescript
interface User {
name: string; age: number; email: string;
}
```

2. Extensibility and Merging

One of the significant differences between types and interfaces is how they handle extensibility. ### Interfaces Are Extensible

Interfaces can be extended using the `extends` keyword, allowing for a clear and hierarchical structure. You can create new interfaces that build upon existing ones:

```typescript
interface Person {
name: string; age: number;
}
interface Employee extends Person { employeeId: number;
}
```

Moreover, interfaces are capable of declaration merging, meaning if you declare the same interface multiple times, TypeScript will merge these declarations into a single interface.

```typescript
interface User {
name: string;
}
interface User { email: string;
}
// Merged User interface const user: User = {
name: 'John Doe',
email: 'john.doe@example.com',
};
```

Types Have Limitations on Extensibility

Types don't support declaration merging. If you attempt to create the same type more than once, it will result in an error. However, types can be combined using intersections:

```typescript
type Person = {
name: string; age: number;
};
type Employee = Person & { employeeId: number;
};
```

In this scenario, while we create `Employee` by extending `Person`, we cannot have multiple declarations for the `Person` type.

80

3. Use Cases for Types vs. Interfaces ### Using Interfaces

Interfaces are generally preferred when defining the shape of objects, especially in codebases that leverage OOP principles. Their ability to extend and merge makes them suitable for defining contracts in larger applications where multiple components might need to adhere to a specific structure.

Using Types

Types, on the other hand, are incredibly versatile and allow for defining complex types that might not just pertain to objects. For example, you can define unions, tuples, and mapped types:

```typescript
type StringOrNumber = string | number; // Union type
type Point = [number, number];  // Tuple type
```

Types might be the better choice when dealing with simpler structures or when combining different types in a more functional style.

4. Performance Considerations

In general performance terms, there is no significant difference between using types and interfaces in TypeScript. However, interfaces can occasionally produce smaller output JavaScript code due to their implicit declaration merging and how they organize type information. This aspect can be noteworthy in larger applications where boilerplate can add up.

Understanding the differences between types and

interfaces in TypeScript is critical for writing robust and maintainable code. While both can achieve similar outcomes, their features, syntactic rules, and use cases differ significantly.

Interfaces excel in scenarios where extensibility and contract definition are paramount, especially for working within frameworks that employ OOP principles. Types shine with their versatility, accommodating complex type constructs that go beyond traditional objects.

Chapter 6: Object-Oriented Programming (OOP) in TypeScript

TypeScript, a superset of JavaScript, brings strong typing and modern features to the OOP style, enhancing code readability, maintainability, and scalability.

6.1 Understanding OOP Concepts

Before diving into OOP with TypeScript, it's essential to understand the fundamental concepts of OOP:

Classes: A blueprint for creating objects. Classes encapsulate data for the object and methods to manipulate that data.

Objects: Instances of classes, holding state and behavior.

Encapsulation: The bundling of data and methods that operate on that data, restricting direct access to some components.

Inheritance: A mechanism for creating a new class based on an existing class. The new class inherits properties and methods from the parent class, enabling code reuse.

Polymorphism: The ability to present the same interface for different underlying forms (data types). It allows methods to do different things based on the object it is acting on.

Abstraction: The concept of hiding the complex reality while exposing only the necessary parts. It helps in reducing programming complexity and increases efficiency of code.

6.2 Defining Classes in TypeScript

In TypeScript, classes are defined using the `class` keyword. Here is a simple example:

```typescript
class Person {

name: string; age: number;

constructor(name: string, age: number) { this.name = name;

this.age = age;
}

introduce(): string {

return `Hello, my name is ${this.name} and I am ${this.age} years old.`;
}
}

const person1 = new Person("Alice", 30);
console.log(person1.introduce());
```

In the above code, we define a `Person` class with properties `name` and `age`, along with a method

`introduce()`. The `constructor` initializes the class properties. ## 6.3 Encapsulation in TypeScript

Encapsulation is achieved using access modifiers. TypeScript provides three access modifiers: `public`,

`private`, and `protected`.

Public: Can be accessed from anywhere.

Private: Can be accessed only within the class itself.

Protected: Can be accessed within the class and its subclasses. Here's how encapsulation works in TypeScript:

```typescript
class BankAccount { private balance: number;

constructor(initialBalance: number) { this.balance = initialBalance;
}

public deposit(amount: number): void { this.balance += amount;
}

public withdraw(amount: number): void { if (amount > this.balance) {

console.log('Insufficient funds');

} else {

this.balance -= amount; console.log(`Withdrew: $${amount}`);
}
}

public getBalance(): number { return this.balance;
}
}

const account = new BankAccount(1000);
```

```
account.deposit(500); console.log(account.getBalance());
//          1500          account.withdraw(300);
console.log(account.getBalance()); // 1200
```
``` ` ` `

In this example, `balance` is a private property, which means it cannot be accessed directly from outside the

`BankAccount` class. We expose the functionality to deposit, withdraw, and check the balance using public methods.

6.4 Inheritance in TypeScript

Inheritance allows a class to inherit properties and methods from another class. This promotes code reuse and establishes a relationship between classes.

Here's an example:

```typescript
class Employee extends Person { employeeId: number;

constructor(name: string, age: number, employeeId: number) { super(name, age);

this.employeeId = employeeId;

}

introduce(): string {

return super.introduce() + ` My employee ID is ${this.employeeId}.`;

}

}

const employee1 = new Employee("Bob", 28, 123);
```
```

```typescript
console.log(employee1.introduce());
```

In this example, `Employee` extends `Person`, inheriting its properties and methods while adding new functionality. The `introduce()` method is overridden to include the employee ID.

6.5 Polymorphism in TypeScript

Polymorphism allows methods to use objects of various types at different times. In TypeScript, this can be achieved through method overriding and interface implementation.

Below is a demonstration using interfaces:

```typescript
interface Shape {

area(): number;

}

class Rectangle implements Shape {

constructor(private width: number, private height: number) {}

area(): number {

return this.width * this.height;

}

}

class Circle implements Shape { constructor(private radius: number) {}

area(): number {

return Math.PI * this.radius * this.radius;
```

```typescript
}
}
const shapes: Shape[] = [new Rectangle(4, 5), new Circle(3)];

shapes.forEach((shape)    =>    {    console.log(`Area: ${shape.area()}`);
});
```

In this example, both `Rectangle` and `Circle` implement the `Shape` interface, thus providing their version of the `area()` method. This shows polymorphism in action: the same method call behaves differently depending on the object type.

6.6 Abstraction in TypeScript

Abstraction can be achieved through abstract classes and interfaces. An abstract class can define methods that must be implemented by derived classes, focusing on the essential characteristics while hiding complex implementations.

Here's an example:

```typescript
abstract class Animal { abstract sound(): string;

makeSound(): void { console.log(this.sound());
}
}
class Dog extends Animal { sound(): string {
```

```
return 'Woof!';
}
}
class Cat extends Animal { sound(): string {
return 'Meow!';
}
}
const animals: Animal[] = [new Dog(), new Cat()];
animals.forEach((animal) => {
animal.makeSound();
});
```
```

In this example, `Animal` is an abstract class that contains an abstract method `sound()` that must be implemented in derived classes. The `makeSound()` method provides common functionality while allowing subclasses to provide specific implementations.

Understanding and utilizing OOP principles in TypeScript will not only streamline your development process but also prepare you for building large-scale applications with efficiency and ease.

## Classes, Properties, and Methods

In this chapter, we will delve into the fundamentals of classes, properties, and methods in TypeScript, demonstrating how these features can help you create
```

more structured and maintainable code.

Introduction to Classes

Classes in TypeScript serve as blueprints for creating objects. They allow developers to encapsulate data and behavior into a single entity, promoting a clean and dependable code structure. The class syntax in TypeScript closely resembles that of ES6 JavaScript, but it adds static typing and additional features that improve code quality.

Defining a Class

To define a class, you use the `class` keyword followed by the class name and then define its properties and methods within curly braces. Here's a simple example:

```typescript
class Car {
// Properties
make: string;
model: string;
year: number;
// Constructor
constructor(make: string, model: string, year: number) {
this.make = make;
this.model = model;
this.year = year;
}
// Method
displayInfo(): string {
return `${this.year} ${this.make} ${this.model}`;
}
}
```

In this example, the `Car` class has three properties: `make`, `model`, and `year`. The constructor initializes these properties when an object of the class is created. The `displayInfo` method returns a string containing the details of the car.

Properties in Classes

Properties in TypeScript classes are essentially the variables or attributes that define the state of an object. TypeScript allows us to assign specific types to properties, ensuring type safety and reducing runtime errors.

Property Modifiers

TypeScript provides access modifiers that you can use to control the visibility of properties:

Public: The default access level; properties are accessible from anywhere.

Private: Properties are accessible only within the class they are defined in.

Protected: Properties are accessible within the class and by inheriting classes.

Here's an example of using access modifiers:

```typescript
class Person {

public name: string; private age: number;

protected profession: string;

constructor(name: string, age: number, profession: string) { this.name = name;

this.age = age; this.profession = profession;

}

public getAge(): number { return this.age;
```

```
}
}
```
```

In this `Person` class, `name` is public, `age` is private, and `profession` is protected. The method `getAge()` is public, allowing external access to the private `age` property.

### Readonly Properties

You can declare properties as `readonly`, preventing them from being modified after the object has been constructed.

```typescript
class Product {

readonly id: number; readonly name: string;

constructor(id: number, name: string) { this.id = id;

this.name = name;

}
}
```

In this case, `id` and `name` cannot be reassigned after the `Product` object is created. ## Methods in Classes

Methods define the behavior of objects created from a class. They can manipulate or provide access to an object's properties and can accept parameters and return values.

Defining Methods
```

Methods are defined similar to functions, with the addition of the `this` keyword to refer to the instance of the class.

```typescript
class Calculator {
add(a: number, b: number): number { return a + b;
}
subtract(a: number, b: number): number { return a - b;
}
}
const calc = new Calculator(); console.log(calc.add(5, 3));
// Output: 8
console.log(calc.subtract(5, 3)); // Output: 2
```

Static Methods

Static methods belong to the class itself rather than any object instance. They are defined with the `static` keyword and can be called without creating an instance of the class.

```typescript
class MathUtils {
static multiply(a: number, b: number): number { return a * b;
}
}
console.log(MathUtils.multiply(4, 5)); // Output: 20
```

Method Overloading

TypeScript supports method overloading, allowing you to define multiple signatures for a method with the same name but different parameters.

```typescript
class Display {
  show(data: string): void; // Overload signature
  show(data: number): void; // Overload signature
  show(data: any): void { // Implementation signature
    console.log(data);
  }
}

const display = new Display();

display.show("Hello, TypeScript!"); // Output: Hello, TypeScript!
display.show(123); // Output: 123
```

Understanding classes, properties, and methods in TypeScript is crucial for writing clean, organized, and type-safe code. Classes provide a foundation for object-oriented programming, enabling developers to create reusable and modular components. By leveraging properties and methods, we can encapsulate data and behavior effectively.

Inheritance, Access Modifiers, and Abstract Classes

TypeScript, a superset of JavaScript, provides robust support for OOP principles, including inheritance, access modifiers, and abstract classes. This chapter will explore these concepts in detail, illustrating how they can be utilized to create organized, maintainable, and scalable code.

1. Inheritance

Inheritance is a fundamental concept in OOP that allows a class (known as a child or derived class) to inherit properties and methods from another class (known as a parent or base class). This promotes code reuse and establishes a natural hierarchy between classes.

In TypeScript, inheritance is achieved using the `extends` keyword. This enables the child class to access all the public and protected members of the parent class.

Example of Inheritance

```typescript
class Animal {
constructor(public name: string) {}
speak(): void {
console.log(`${this.name} makes a noise.`);
}
}
class Dog extends Animal { speak(): void {
console.log(`${this.name} barks.`);
}
}
const dog = new Dog("Buddy"); dog.speak(); // Output:
Buddy barks.
```

```
```

In the above example, the `Dog` class inherits from the `Animal` class. It overrides the `speak` method of the parent class to provide a more specific implementation. This shows how inheritance allows us to extend and customize functionality in derived classes.

2. Access Modifiers

Access modifiers control the visibility and accessibility of class members (properties and methods). TypeScript provides three access modifiers:

public: Members are accessible from anywhere.

private: Members are only accessible within the class they are declared in.

protected: Members are accessible within the class and by derived classes.

Using access modifiers helps enforce encapsulation, where internal state and behavior are kept hidden from outside manipulation.

Example of Access Modifiers

```typescript
class Person {

public name: string; private age: number; protected email: string;

constructor(name: string, age: number, email: string) {
this.name = name;

this.age = age; this.email = email;

}
```

```typescript
public getDetails(): string {
return `${this.name}, Age: ${this.age}`;
}
}
class Employee extends Person { private employeeId: number;
constructor(name: string, age: number, email: string, employeeId: number) { super(name, age, email);
this.employeeId = employeeId;
}
public getEmployeeDetails(): string {
return `${this.getDetails()}, Email: ${this.email}, Employee ID: ${this.employeeId}`;
}
}
const employee = new Employee("Alice", 30, "alice@example.com", 101);
console.log(employee.getEmployeeDetails()); // Output: Alice, Age: 30, Email: alice@example.com, Employee ID: 101
```

In this example, the `age` member is private and cannot be accessed directly outside the `Person` class, while the `email` member is protected and is accessible in the `Employee` class thanks to inheritance.

3. Abstract Classes

Abstract classes are classes that cannot be instantiated directly but can be subclassed. They allow you to define abstract methods, which must be implemented in derived classes. Abstract classes are useful for providing a base structure while enforcing certain behaviors in subclasses.

To define an abstract class in TypeScript, you use the `abstract` keyword. When a class contains at least one abstract method, it must also be marked as abstract.

Example of Abstract Classes

```typescript
abstract class Shape { constructor(public color: string) {}

abstract area(): number; public toString(): string {

return `Shape color: ${this.color}`;

}
}
class Circle extends Shape {

constructor(color: string, public radius: number) {
super(color);

}
area(): number {

return Math.PI * this.radius ** 2;

}
}
class Rectangle extends Shape {

constructor(color: string, public width: number, public height: number) { super(color);
```

```
}
area(): number {
return this.width * this.height;
}
}
const circle = new Circle("red", 5);
console.log(`${circle.toString()}, Area: ${circle.area()}`);
// Output: Shape color: red, Area: 78.53981633974483
const rectangle = new Rectangle("blue", 10, 5);
console.log(`${rectangle.toString()},                Area:
${rectangle.area()}`); // Output: Shape color: blue, Area:
50
```
```

In this case, the `Shape` class serves as an abstract base class, defining the structure of shape-related classes. Each subclass, `Circle` and `Rectangle`, implements the `area` method, providing specific functionality for different shapes.

By leveraging these features, TypeScript developers can create more sophisticated and structured applications, ultimately leading to improved code quality and developer productivity.
```

Chapter 7: Advanced TypeScript Types

In this chapter, we will explore the advanced features of TypeScript type system that allow developers to create more robust and maintainable applications. TypeScript enhances JavaScript by introducing static types that can help prevent many common errors developers face. By leveraging advanced types, we can create more complex and reusable code structures.

Table of Contents

1. Introduction to Advanced Types

TypeScript's type system is incredibly flexible and powerful. While basic types such as `string`, `number`, and `boolean` are essential, advanced types allow you to build more complex structures. In web development, where APIs and data structures can vary widely, these features become invaluable.

2. Union Types

Union types allow you to define a variable that can hold more than one type. This is especially useful for functions that might return different value types based on input conditions.

```typescript
function logId(id: string | number) { console.log(`The ID is: ${id}`);
}

logId(101); // The ID is: 101 logId('202'); // The ID is: 202
```

In the example above, the `logId` function can accept both strings and numbers as its argument. TypeScript will ensure that the passed argument is one of the specified types.

3. Intersection Types

Intersection types allow you to combine multiple types into one. This means that you can create a type that has the properties of all the types it combines.

```typescript interface User {
name: string; age: number;
}

interface Account { accountId: string; balance: number;
}

type UserAccount = User & Account; const userAccount: UserAccount = {
name: "Alice", age: 30,
```

```
accountId: "A123", balance: 1000,
};
```

Here, the `UserAccount` type combines properties from both `User` and `Account`, indicating that it possesses all fields from both types.

4. Type Guards

Type guards are functions or expressions that check the type of a variable at runtime. They help the TypeScript compiler narrow down the type of a variable, enabling more specific type checks.

```typescript
function printValue(value: string | number) { if (typeof value === "string") {
console.log(`String value: ${value}`);
} else {
console.log(`Number value: ${value}`);
}
}
```

In this example, the `typeof` operator is used as a type guard to determine if the `value` is a string or a number. This allows the compiler to infer the type correctly within the respective branches.

5. Mapped Types

Mapped types allow you to create new types by

transforming properties of an existing type. This feature is particularly useful when you want to create variations of a type without rewriting it.

```typescript
type ReadOnly<T> = { readonly [P in keyof T]: T[P];
};
interface User { name: string; age: number;
}
type ReadOnlyUser = ReadOnly<User>;
const user: ReadOnlyUser = { name: "Bob",
age: 25,
};
// user.age = 26; // Error: Cannot assign to 'age' because it is a read-only property.
```

In this example, the `ReadOnly` type takes an existing type and creates a new one where all properties are read-only.

6. Conditional Types

Conditional types offer a powerful way to create types that depend on a condition. They are expressed using the syntax `A extends B ? C : D`.

```typescript
type IsString<T> = T extends string ? "Yes" : "No";
type Result1 = IsString<string>; // "Yes" type Result2 = IsString<number>; // "No"
```

```
```

Here, `IsString` is a conditional type that checks if `T` extends `string`. This flexibility allows developers to create types based on other types dynamically.

7. Utility Types

TypeScript comes with several built-in utility types to help with common type transformations. Some of the most useful ones include `Partial`, `Required`, `Readonly`, `Record`, and `Pick`.

`Partial<T>` makes all properties of `T` optional.

`Required<T>` makes all properties of `T` required.

`Readonly<T>` makes all properties of `T` read-only.

`Record<K, T>` constructs an object type with specific property keys of type `K` and values of type `T`.

`Pick<T, K>` creates a type by picking a set of properties `K` from `T`.

```typescript
interface User {

name: string; age: number; email?: string;

}

type PartialUser = Partial<User>; // All properties are optional

type RequiredEmailUser = Required<Pick<User, 'email'>>; // 'email' is required
```

8. Template Literal Types

Template literal types bring the power of string templates

to the type system, allowing you to create strings that follow a particular pattern.

```typescript
type EventName = 'click' | 'mouseover';

type EventAction<T extends string> = `on${Capitalize<T>}`;

type ClickEvent = EventAction<'click'>; // "onClick"

type MouseOverEvent = EventAction<'mouseover'>; // "onMouseover"
```

In the example above, `EventAction` uses a template literal type to generate specific names based on a given string type.

Advanced types in TypeScript provide robust tools for managing complex data structures and applying strong typing to improve code reliability. Mastering these types not only enhances your development skills but also contributes to building scalable applications.

Union, Intersection, and Literal Types

TypeScript enhances JavaScript with static typing and brings along powerful type constructs, two of which are union and intersection types. Additionally, literal types add a layer of specificity that can be incredibly useful in certain scenarios. In this chapter, we will explore these constructs in detail, demonstrating their utility with examples and best practices.

1. Union Types

Union types allow you to define a variable that can hold values of multiple types. This is particularly useful when a function or data structure can accept different types, giving you flexibility while maintaining strong typing.

1.1 Syntax

A union type is defined using the pipe (`|`) symbol. The basic syntax looks like this:

```typescript
let value: string | number;
```

In this example, the variable `value` can hold either a string or a number. #### 1.2 Example

Let's consider a function that can take either a string or a number:

```typescript
function printValue(value: string | number): void {
console.log(`The value is: ${value}`);
}

printValue("Hello, TypeScript!"); // The value is: Hello,
TypeScript! printValue(42);          // The value is: 42
```

In the example above, `printValue` can handle both string and number inputs, demonstrating the utility of union types in creating versatile functions.

1.3 Type Guards

When working with union types, TypeScript's type guards help determine the specific type of a variable at runtime.

```typescript
function processValue(value: string | number) { if (typeof value === "string") {

console.log(`String value: ${value.toUpperCase()}`);

} else {

console.log(`Number value: ${value.toFixed(2)}`);

}

}

processValue("hello");    //    String    value:    HELLO
processValue(3.14); // Number value: 3.14
```

Here, `typeof` acts as a type guard, allowing TypeScript to infer the exact type of `value`, thereby providing access to type-specific methods without any errors.

2. Intersection Types

While union types enable variables to accept multiple types, intersection types allow you to combine multiple types into one. This means that an intersection type retains all characteristics from its constituent types.

2.1 Syntax

An intersection type is defined using the ampersand (`&`) symbol. The syntax looks like this:

```typescript
type Person = { name: string };
```

```typescript
type Employee = { employeeId: number };
type EmployeeDetails = Person & Employee;
```

In this example, `EmployeeDetails` is an intersection type that contains both `name` and `employeeId`. #### 2.2 Example

Let's consider a scenario with a function that requires an object with properties from both `Person` and `Employee`:

```typescript
function printEmployeeDetails(details: EmployeeDetails) { console.log(`Name: ${details.name}, Employee ID: ${details.employeeId}`);
}
const employee = { name: "Jane Doe", employeeId: 12345 };
printEmployeeDetails(employee); // Name: Jane Doe, Employee ID: 12345
```

As shown, `printEmployeeDetails` expects an object that conforms to both `Person` and `Employee`, ensuring robust type-checking.

3. Literal Types

Literal types in TypeScript allow you to specify the exact value of a string, number, or boolean type. This enhances type safety by enforcing specific values that can be assigned to variables.

3.1 Syntax

Literal types can be defined as follows:

```typescript
let status: "success" | "error" | "pending";
```

In this example, the `status` variable can only hold one of the specified string literal values. #### 3.2 Example

Let's demonstrate a function that takes a literal type:

```typescript
function setStatus(status: "success" | "error" | "pending") {
console.log(`Current status: ${status}`);
}
setStatus("success");    // Current status: success
setStatus("error");   // Current status: error
// setStatus("unknown"); // Error: Argument of type
"'unknown'" is not assignable to parameter of type
"'success" | "error" | "pending"'.
```

In this example, calling `setStatus` with any string other than the specified literals leads to a compiler error, enhancing type safety.

4. Combining Constructs

One of the powerful features of TypeScript is the ability to combine union types, intersection types, and literal types.

This allows you to define complex types with high specificity.

4.1 Example

Let's combine these constructs:

```typescript
type ResponseStatus = "success" | "error";

interface ApiResponse { status: ResponseStatus; data?:
string | null;
}

function handleApiResponse(response: ApiResponse) { if
(response.status === "success") {

console.log(`Data received: ${response.data}`);

} else {

console.log("An error occurred.");

}

}

handleApiResponse({ status: "success", data: "User data"
}); handleApiResponse({ status: "error" });
```

In this case, we've defined an `ApiResponse` interface using union and literal types together, enabling us to specify the exact shape of the data we expect.

Understanding union types, intersection types, and literal types in TypeScript can significantly enhance your programming capabilities. These constructs not only provide flexibility and power in type definitions but also strengthen the safety and readability of your code. They enable you to capture the intent of your programs more effectively, paving the way for robust applications suited for today's development needs.

Type Assertions and Type Guards

This chapter delves into the concepts of type assertions and type guards, illustrates their differences, and demonstrates how to implement them in TypeScript.

Understanding Type Assertions

Type assertions are a way of telling the TypeScript compiler, "I know better than you about the type of this variable." This feature is particularly useful when TypeScript cannot infer the type correctly or when working with dynamic content such as JSON or data from APIs. Type assertions do not perform any runtime checks; they are solely a compile-time construct that allows developers to provide more information about types.

Syntax of Type Assertions

There are primarily two syntaxes for creating a type assertion in TypeScript:

The angle-bracket syntax:

```typescript
let someValue: unknown = "this is a string";

let strLength: number = (<string>someValue).length;
```

```
```

The as syntax:

```typescript
let someValue: unknown = "this is another string";  let strLength: number = (someValue as string).length;
```

Both methods achieve the same result, with the `as` syntax being more common and recommended, especially when used in JSX contexts where angle brackets may not be valid.

When to Use Type Assertions

Type assertions should be used with care. They can introduce risks if misused, as they override TypeScript's type checking. Here are some common scenarios where type assertions are beneficial:

When dealing with third-party libraries: If you have a library that lacks TypeScript definitions, you may assert the type of an imported object.

When accessing properties of an object with a known structure but without fully defined types. ### Example of Type Assertion

Consider the following example where we are working with an API response that is initially of type

`unknown`:

```typescript interface User {
```

id: number;

username: string;

```typescript
}
function getUser(): unknown {
return JSON.parse('{"id": 1, "username": "JohnDoe"}');
}
let userData = getUser(); let user = userData as User;
console.log(user.username); // JohnDoe
```

In this case, we use type assertions to let TypeScript know that the output of `getUser()` matches the `User` interface.

Understanding Type Guards

Type guards, on the other hand, are a way of narrowing down the type of a variable at runtime. They allow you to perform checks on types dynamically and ensure that your code behaves as expected based on the current type.

Common Type Guards

Type guards can be implemented in several ways:

Using `typeof` Operator:

The `typeof` operator can be used to check primitive types.

```typescript
function printValue(value: number | string) { if (typeof value === "string") {
console.log(value.toUpperCase());
} else {
```

```
    console.log(value);
  }
}
```
```

**Using `instanceof` Operator:**

The `instanceof` operator can be used to check object types.

```typescript
class Dog { bark() {
    console.log("Woof!");
  }
}
class Cat { meow() {
    console.log("Meow!");
  }
}
function makeSound(animal: Dog | Cat) { if (animal instanceof Dog) {
    animal.bark();
  } else {
    animal.meow();
  }
}
```

User-Defined Type Guards:
```

You can create custom type guard functions that return a type predicate.

```typescript
typescript interface Fish {

swim(): void;

}

interface Bird { fly(): void;

}

function isFish(animal: Fish | Bird): animal is Fish {
return (animal as Fish).swim !== undefined;

}

function move(animal: Fish | Bird) { if (isFish(animal)) {

animal.swim();

} else {

animal.fly();

}

}
```

Benefits of Type Guards

Type guards provide several benefits in TypeScript:

Type Safety: They ensure that you access properties or methods only on the correct type, avoiding runtime errors.

Clarity: They improve code readability by clearly defining paths based on the types.

Maintainability: They facilitate adding new types or properties without breaking existing types.

Understanding how and when to use these features can greatly enhance the robustness of TypeScript applications, making your code safer, clearer, and easier to maintain.

Chapter 8: Handling Asynchronous Programming in TypeScript

TypeScript, which builds upon JavaScript, offers several powerful features to handle asynchronous programming effectively. In this chapter, we'll explore the main concepts of asynchronous programming in TypeScript, including Promises, async/await syntax, and various patterns to manage asynchronous operations.

Understanding Asynchronous Programming

The asynchronous nature of JavaScript means that certain tasks can run concurrently, allowing other tasks to continue executing without waiting for the completion of those tasks. This is particularly important for I/O operations and data fetching, which can take an unpredictable amount of time to complete.

The Event Loop and Callbacks

At the core of JavaScript's asynchronous capabilities is the event loop, which facilitates the handling of callbacks. A callback is a function that gets called after a certain task completes. However, managing multiple callbacks can lead to complications, including "callback hell" — a situation where callbacks are nested within other callbacks, making the code difficult to read and maintain.

For illustration:

```typescript
function fetchData(callback: (data: string) => void) {
setTimeout(() => {

callback("Fetched Data");
```

```
}, 2000);
}
fetchData((data) => {
console.log(data); // Output after 2 seconds
});
```
```

While the above example illustrates the use of a callback, it quickly becomes unwieldy as the number of dependent asynchronous operations increases.

## Promises

To improve the readability of asynchronous code, JavaScript introduced Promises, which represent the completion (or failure) of an asynchronous operation and its resulting value. A Promise can be in one of three states: pending, fulfilled, or rejected.

### Creating and Handling Promises

Here's how you can create and use Promises in TypeScript:

```typescript
function fetchData(): Promise<string> {
return new Promise((resolve, reject) => { setTimeout(()
=> {
const success = true; // Simulate success or failure if
(success) {
resolve("Fetched Data");
} else {
```
```

```typescript
    reject(new Error("Failed to fetch data"));
    }
}, 2000);
});
}
fetchData()
.then((data) => console.log(data)) // Output after 2
seconds
.catch((error) => console.error(error));
```

In the example, `fetchData` returns a Promise, allowing us to handle successful data fetching or an error in a more manageable way than callbacks.

Async/Await Syntax

TypeScript leverages the async/await syntax, which is syntactic sugar over Promises, making asynchronous code easier to read and write. An async function always returns a Promise, and the await keyword can be used to pause the execution of the function until the Promise is resolved.

Using Async/Await

Consider the previous example rewritten with async/await:

```typescript
async function fetchDataAsync(): Promise<string> {
return new Promise((resolve) => {

setTimeout(() => { resolve("Fetched Data");
```

```typescript
}, 2000);
});
}
async function getData() { try {

const data = await fetchDataAsync(); // Waits for the
Promise to resolve console.log(data); // Output after 2
seconds

} catch (error) { console.error(error);
}
}
getData();
```
```
` ` `
```

In this case, the `getData` function is declared as async, allowing us to use await to pause execution until

`fetchDataAsync` resolves. This linear flow of execution mimics synchronous code, greatly enhancing readability.

Error Handling in Asynchronous Code

Error handling in asynchronous programming is crucial for robust applications. With Promises, you can use the `.catch()` method to handle rejections. In async/await code, try/catch blocks are used to catch errors, making it easier to manage unexpected situations.

Example of Error Handling:

```typescript
async function fetchWithError(): Promise<string> {
return new Promise((resolve, reject) => {
```

```typescript
  setTimeout(() => {
    reject(new Error("An error occurred"));
  }, 2000);
  });
}
async function handleData() { try {
  const data = await fetchWithError(); // This will throw an error console.log(data);
} catch (error) {
  console.error("Error:", error.message); // Handle error here
  }
}
handleData();
```

Chaining Promises

One powerful feature Promises provide is chaining. You can return a new Promise from the `.then()` method, allowing multiple asynchronous operations to be performed in sequence.

Chaining Example:

```typescript
function stepOne(): Promise<string> { return new Promise((resolve) => {
  setTimeout(() => resolve("Step One Complete"), 1000);
```

```
});
}
function stepTwo(input: string): Promise<string> { return
new Promise((resolve) => {

setTimeout(()  =>  resolve(`${input}  -  Step  Two
Complete`), 1000);

});
}
stepOne()
.then(stepTwo)
.then((result) => console.log(result)); // Chained output
after 2 seconds
```
    ` ` `

Handling asynchronous programming in TypeScript is
streamlined through the use of Promises and async/await
syntax. These tools enable developers to write cleaner,
more manageable code while maintaining the
asynchronous capabilities of JavaScript.

Promises and Async/Await in TypeScript

This chapter will explore these fundamental concepts,
their implementation in TypeScript, and how they provide
a more manageable way to write asynchronous code.

Understanding Promises

Before diving into async/await, it's crucial to understand what a Promise is. A Promise is an object that represents the eventual completion (or failure) of an asynchronous operation and its resulting value. It can be in one of three states:

Pending: The initial state, neither fulfilled nor rejected.

Fulfilled: The asynchronous operation completed successfully, resulting in a value.

Rejected: The asynchronous operation failed, resulting in a reason for the failure. ### Creating a Promise

In TypeScript, creating a Promise involves using the `Promise` constructor. The constructor takes a function called the executor, which has two parameters: `resolve` and `reject`, used to settle the Promise.

```typescript
const myPromise = new Promise<string>((resolve, reject) => { const success = true; // Simulating an operation

if (success) {

resolve("Operation was successful!");

} else {

reject("Operation failed!");

}

});
```

In this example, `myPromise` is a Promise that resolves to

a string. ### Using Promises

To handle the outcome of a Promise, we use the `.then()` method for fulfillment and `.catch()` for errors. This chainable syntax facilitates a clean flow of asynchronous operations.

```typescript
myPromise
.then(result => {
console.log(result); // Output: Operation was successful!
})
.catch(error => { console.error(error);
});
```

Chaining Promises

One of the powerful features of Promises is their ability to chain multiple asynchronous operations. Each `.then()` returns a new Promise, allowing you to perform sequential asynchronous tasks.

```typescript
const fetchData = (): Promise<string> => {
// Simulate fetching data
return new Promise<string>((resolve) => { setTimeout(() => resolve("Fetched data"), 1000);
});
};
```

```typescript
fetchData()
.then(data => {
console.log(data); // Output: Fetched data
return "Processed " + data; // Return a new value
})
.then(result => {
console.log(result); // Output: Processed Fetched data
});
```

Error Handling in Promises

Error handling can be effectively managed by using the `.catch()` method at the end of the chain. This centralizes error handling, making asynchronous logic easier to read and debug.

```typescript
fetchData()
.then(data => {
throw new Error("An error occurred!"); // Forcing an error
})
.catch(error => {
console.error(error.message); // Output: An error occurred!
});
```

The Async/Await Syntax

Although Promises provide a good way to handle asynchronous operations, the async/await syntax offers an even cleaner and more intuitive approach. Introduced in ES2017, async/await enables you to write asynchronous code that looks synchronous, simplifying the code structure.

Declaring Async Functions

An `async` function is a function declared with the `async` keyword. It always returns a Promise. Regardless of the return value, the function wraps it in a Promise, allowing for easier chaining.

```typescript
const fetchDataAsync = async (): Promise<string> => {
return "Fetched data asynchronously";

};
```

Using Await

The `await` keyword can only be used inside an `async` function. It pauses the execution of the function until the Promise is resolved or rejected. This makes the code cleaner and easier to follow.

```typescript
const fetchDataWithAwait = async () => { try {

const result = await fetchData(); // Awaiting the Promise
console.log(result); // Output: Fetched data

} catch (error) { console.error("Error:", error);
```

```
}
};
fetchDataWithAwait();
```
```
```

In this example, the function `fetchDataWithAwait` retrieves data and logs it, while handling any potential errors in a straightforward manner.

Error Handling with Async/Await

Error handling in async/await can be done using the `try...catch` block, providing a clear and intuitive way to manage errors that may arise during asynchronous operations.

```typescript
const fetchDataWithErrorHandling = async () => { try {

const data = await fetchData();

throw new Error("Simulated error!");

} catch (error) {

console.error("Caught an error:", error.message); // Output: Caught an error: Simulated error!

}
};
```
```

## Advantages of Async/Await

Using async/await in TypeScript and JavaScript has several advantages:
```

Readability: The code is easier to read and understand as it resembles synchronous code.

Error Handling: Errors can be caught using `try...catch`, making it simpler than chaining `.catch()` methods.

Debugging: Stack traces in async/await are easier to follow than in Promise chains.

We explored how Promises provide a way to handle asynchronous operations and the syntactic sugar that async/await brings to simplify code management. Asynchronous programming can often make or break applications, and mastering these tools will greatly enhance your ability to develop performant, user-friendly applications.

Working with Fetch API and Axios

This chapter covers two popular methods for making HTTP requests in TypeScript: the native Fetch API and the Axios library. Both approaches provide robust functionalities, but they come with different strengths and nuances. By the end of this chapter, you will have a solid understanding of how to use both tools in your TypeScript projects.

Understanding Fetch API

The Fetch API is a built-in JavaScript feature that provides a modern way to make API calls. It is promise-based, making it easier to work with asynchronous operations. Here's how to use the Fetch API in TypeScript.

Basic Usage of Fetch

To get started with Fetch, you can call `fetch()` with the API endpoint as an argument. The basic syntax is as follows:

```typescript
fetch(url)
.then(response => { if (!response.ok) {

throw new Error('Network response was not ok');

}

return response.json();

})

.then(data => console.log(data))

.catch(error => console.error('There has been a problem with your fetch operation:', error));
```

Type Safety with Fetch API

To leverage TypeScript's type safety, it's essential to define the types for the data you expect from the API:

```typescript
interface User { id: number; name: string;
email: string;

}

async function fetchUsers(): Promise<User[]> {

const response = await fetch('https://api.example.com/users'); if (!response.ok) {

throw new Error('Network response was not ok');

}
```

```typescript
  return await response.json();
}
fetchUsers()
.then(users => console.log(users))
.catch(error => console.error('Fetch error:', error));
```

Making POST Requests with Fetch

You can also use the Fetch API to send data to a server using a POST request. Here's an example:

```typescript
async function createUser(user: User): Promise<User> {
const       response       =       await
fetch('https://api.example.com/users', { method: 'POST',
headers: {
'Content-Type': 'application/json',
},
body: JSON.stringify(user),
});

if (!response.ok) {
throw new Error('Network response was not ok');
}

return await response.json();
```

```typescript
}
const newUser: User = { id: 0, name: 'John Doe', email: 'johndoe@example.com' }; createUser(newUser)

.then(user => console.log('Created user:', user))

.catch(error => console.error('Error creating user:', error));
```

Introduction to Axios

Axios is a popular library for making HTTP requests, built on top of the XMLHttpRequest API. It simplifies the API interaction, providing an easier syntax and additional features like interceptors and request cancellation.

Installing Axios

First, you need to install Axios in your TypeScript project:

```bash
npm install axios
```

Basic Usage of Axios

Using Axios is straightforward. Here's how to make a GET request:

```typescript
import axios from 'axios';

async function fetchUsers(): Promise<User[]> {

const response = await axios.get<User[]>('https://api.example.com/users');
return response.data;
```

```
}
fetchUsers()
.then(users => console.log(users))
.catch(error => console.error('Axios error:', error));
```

Type Safety with Axios

Just like with Fetch, you can define the response type when using Axios to ensure type safety:

```typescript
interface User { id: number; name: string; email: string;
}
async function fetchUsers(): Promise<User[]> {
const response = await axios.get<User[]>('https://api.example.com/users');
return response.data;
}
```

Making POST Requests with Axios

To send data with Axios, you can use the following:

```typescript
async function createUser(user: User): Promise<User> {
const response = await axios.post<User>('https://api.example.com/users', user);
return response.data;
}
```

```typescript
const newUser: User = { id: 0, name: 'Jane Doe', email:
'janedoe@example.com' }; createUser(newUser)

.then(user => console.log('Created user:', user))

.catch(error => console.error('Error creating user:',
error));
```

Advanced Features of Axios

One of the benefits of Axios is its ability to intercept requests or responses. This can be particularly useful for tasks such as logging or modifying requests globally:

```typescript
axios.interceptors.request.use(config => {
console.log('Request:', config);

return config;

}, error => {

return Promise.reject(error);

});

axios.interceptors.response.use(response         =>         {
console.log('Response:', response);

return response;

}, error => {

return Promise.reject(error);

});
```

Both the Fetch API and Axios provide powerful options for making HTTP requests in TypeScript. Fetch is a built-in modern approach that is lightweight and

133

straightforward, while Axios offers additional features and a more user-friendly interface.

Chapter 10: TypeScript and JavaScript Interoperability

TypeScript, designed as a superset of JavaScript, allows developers to write code with static types, providing an enhanced toolset for building robust applications. However, developers often face scenarios where TypeScript and JavaScript must coexist. This chapter delves into the principles of interoperability between TypeScript and JavaScript, offering practical insights and strategies for leveraging both languages effectively in a project.

9.1 Understanding the Interoperability Between TypeScript and JavaScript

TypeScript was designed to embrace JavaScript, which means it naturally supports all JavaScript features. This intercompatibility allows developers to gradually adopt TypeScript's benefits without rewriting entire codebases. JavaScript code can be included in TypeScript projects, and TypeScript can output JavaScript that is compatible with various versions of the ECMAScript standard.

9.1.1 TypeScript's Type System

TypeScript enhances JavaScript with a powerful type system that helps catch errors at compile time rather than at runtime. While JavaScript allows dynamic typing, TypeScript enforces type annotations, providing a clearer structure for code and improving maintainability. This feature is crucial when integrating JavaScript libraries into TypeScript projects, as it allows developers to define the types expected from these libraries, reducing the likelihood of runtime errors.

9.2 Integrating JavaScript into TypeScript

One of the significant advantages of TypeScript is its ability to seamlessly integrate existing JavaScript code. When working with a project that includes both TypeScript and JavaScript files, the following considerations should be kept in mind:

9.2.1 Creating Type Definitions

To use JavaScript libraries in a TypeScript project, developers often need to create Type Definitions. Type Definitions tell TypeScript about the structure and types of the JavaScript code being imported. This can be done manually or by using DefinitelyTyped, a community-driven repository containing type definitions for external libraries.

Example 9.2.1: Defining a Type for a JavaScript Library

```typescript
// custom-library.d.ts

declare module 'custom-library' {

export function greet(name: string): string;

}

// Using the library in a TypeScript file import { greet } from 'custom-library';

const message: string = greet('World');
console.log(message); // Outputs: Hello, World!
```

```
```

9.2.2 Using Any and Unknown Types

When the types of JavaScript code are uncertain, TypeScript allows the use of `any` and `unknown` types. The `any` type disables type checking, giving complete flexibility at the cost of safety. The `unknown` type, however, is safer since it requires type checking before performing operations on the variable.

9.2.3 Enabling TypeScript to Ignore JavaScript

In some cases, developers might prefer to keep certain JavaScript files free of TypeScript's strict type checking. By setting `allowJs` to `true` in the `tsconfig.json` file, TypeScript can parse JavaScript files, allowing them to coexist with TypeScript files. Setting `"checkJs": false` will suppress type-checking errors in the JavaScript files.

9.3 Compiling TypeScript to JavaScript

The TypeScript compiler (`tsc`) converts TypeScript code into JavaScript, making it possible to run TypeScript applications in any environment that supports JavaScript. The compilation process includes several important configurations in the `tsconfig.json` file:

9.3.1 Targeting JavaScript Versions

Using the `target` option, developers can specify which version of JavaScript to compile to. This ensures compatibility with various runtimes:

```json
{
"compilerOptions": { "target": "es6"
```

```
}
}
```
` ` `

9.3.2 Module Resolution

TypeScript supports multiple module systems (CommonJS, AMD, ESNext, etc.). The module resolution can be configured using the `module` option in the `tsconfig.json`, which adapts the output for various environments.

9.4 Best Practices for Interoperability

To ensure smooth operation between TypeScript and JavaScript, developers should consider the following best practices:

9.4.1 Progressive Migration

Developers can gradually migrate a JavaScript project to TypeScript by renaming `.js` files to `.ts` or `.jsx` to `.tsx`, and progressively adding type annotations. This strategy minimizes disruptions during the transition and enhances the project incrementally.

9.4.2 Consistent Code Standards

Consistent coding standards promote better collaboration and reduce confusion, especially in mixed projects. Using a linter that supports both JavaScript and TypeScript can maintain uniformity in coding styles, enhancing code readability across the board. ### 9.4.3 Comprehensive Testing

Regardless of whether code is written in JavaScript or TypeScript, rigorous testing is crucial. Implementing testing frameworks like Jest or Mocha can help catch potential issues early, ensuring that both parts of the codebase work as expected.

By following the best practices outlined in this chapter, developers can create a harmonious environment that maximizes productivity while maintaining code quality. As TypeScript continues to evolve, staying updated on the latest features and improvements will further enhance the synergy between these two powerful languages, leading to even more robust software solutions.

Using TypeScript with JavaScript Libraries

This chapter will explore how to effectively use TypeScript in conjunction with JavaScript libraries, demonstrating how to bridge the gap between TypeScript's type system and JavaScript's dynamic nature.

Understanding Type Definitions

One of the most significant advantages of using TypeScript is its strong typing system. To leverage TypeScript effectively with JavaScript libraries, developers need proper type definitions. These type definitions allow TypeScript to understand the structure and types of JavaScript libraries, enabling powerful development features like autocompletion, type checking, and improved documentation.

Type Definition Files

Type definitions for JavaScript libraries are typically provided in `.d.ts` files. These files describe the types and structures used in a library, effectively informing TypeScript how to interact with it.

For example, if you're using a library like Lodash, there are already existing type definitions available. You can install them via npm:

```bash
npm install --save-dev @types/lodash
```

This command installs the type definitions from the DefinitelyTyped repository, allowing TypeScript to understand the types used by Lodash functions.

Creating Your Own Type Definitions

If a library you're using does not have type definitions available, you have the option to create your own. This can be done by creating a `.d.ts` file and manually defining the types you need.

Here's a simple example for a hypothetical library:

```typescript
// myLibrary.d.ts
declare module 'myLibrary' {
export function greet(name: string): string;
}
```

Now, when you import and use `myLibrary`, TypeScript recognizes the `greet` function and its expected parameters.

Using JavaScript Libraries in TypeScript

Integrating a JavaScript library into a TypeScript project can be straightforward. Here are some steps to follow:

Step 1: Install the Library

Start by installing the JavaScript library using npm or yarn. For example, to install Moment.js:

```bash
npm install moment
```

Step 2: Install Type Definitions (if available)

If type definitions exist for the library, install them as shown previously. For Moment.js, you run:

```bash
npm install --save-dev @types/moment
```

Step 3: Import and Use the Library

Once installed, you can use the library in your TypeScript files like so:

```typescript
import moment from 'moment';

const now: string = moment().format('MMMM Do YYYY, h:mm:ss a'); console.log(now);
```

With the type definitions in place, TypeScript will provide type checking and IntelliSense for the Moment.js library.

141

Handling Libraries without Type Definitions

There may be instances where a library does not have available type definitions. In such cases, you can: ### 1. Use `any` Type

If you're in a hurry, you can declare the library with the `any` type. This will bypass type checking, which may not be ideal for larger applications but can be a temporary solution.

```typescript
declare module 'my-untype-library'; import myLib from 'my-untype-library';

const value: any = myLib.someFunction();
```

2. Partial Type Definitions

If you want better type safety, consider writing partial type definitions for only the parts of the library you are using. This can help increase consistency without fully defining everything:

```typescript
declare module 'someLibrary' {

export function importantFunction(param: string): boolean;

}
```

3. Type Assertion

You can use type assertions when you know the type of a

variable you're working with but TypeScript cannot infer it.

```typescript
const myLib = require('my-untype-library') as { myFunction: (arg: string) => number };

const result = myLib.myFunction("test");
```

Real-World Example: Integrating jQuery

Let's say you want to integrate jQuery into a TypeScript application. Here's how you can do it step by step: ### Step 1: Install jQuery

```bash
npm install jquery
```

Step 2: Install Type Definitions

```bash
npm install --save-dev @types/jquery
```

Step 3: Use jQuery in TypeScript

You can now use jQuery with type safety in your TypeScript files:

```typescript
import * as $ from 'jquery';

$(document).ready(() => {

$('#myButton').on('click', () => { alert('Button clicked!');
```

143

```
});

});

` ` `
```

By understanding type definitions, you are better equipped to maintain type safety in your projects. While many libraries come with type definitions out of the box, knowing how to create your own or work with untyped libraries is crucial for harnessing the full potential of TypeScript.

Migrating a JavaScript Project to TypeScript

With its static typing, enhanced tooling support, and clear intent, TypeScript allows developers to write more maintainable and error-free code. Migrating a JavaScript project to TypeScript may seem daunting, but this chapter aims to simplify the process and provide a step-by-step guide to facilitate a smooth transition.

Why Migrate to TypeScript?

Before diving into the migration process, it's essential to understand the advantages of TypeScript over JavaScript:

Static Typing: TypeScript's static type system helps catch errors at compile time rather than at runtime, drastically reducing bugs and improving code quality.

Enhanced Tooling: TypeScript integrates well with IDEs and editors, offering better autocomplete, refactoring tools, and inline documentation.

Improved Collaboration: With strict types, team

members can understand the expected data structures, making collaboration more straightforward.

Better Documentation: Type annotations serve as built-in documentation, making it easier for developers to understand code quickly.

Step-by-Step Migration Process ### Step 1: Set Up Your Environment

Before migrating your project, ensure that you have Node.js and npm installed. Begin by installing TypeScript globally:

```bash

npm install -g typescript
```

Next, initialize a new TypeScript configuration file in the root of your project:

```bash tsc --init
```

This command creates a `tsconfig.json` file that you can customize according to your project needs. ### Step 2: Adjust the `tsconfig.json` File

A basic `tsconfig.json` file is created with several default options. Customize it as follows:

```json
{
"compilerOptions": {
"target": "es6",      // Set the ECMAScript target version
```

```
  "module": "commonjs",        // Set the module
system

  "strict": true, // Enable all strict type-checking options

  "esModuleInterop": true,        //                 Enable
interoperability between CommonJS and ES Modules
  "skipLibCheck": true,      // Skip type checking of
declaration files

  "forceConsistentCasingInFileNames": true // Enforce
consistent file casing

},

"include": ["src/**/*"],       // Specify the files to compile
"exclude": ["node_modules", "**/*.spec.ts"] // Exclude
unnecessary files

}
```
```

### Step 3: Change File Extensions

Start changing your JavaScript files from `.js` to `.ts`. For
React projects, change `.jsx` to `.tsx`. The TypeScript
compiler can handle `.js` files if the `allowJs` option is
set to `true` in the config. However, to fully leverage
TypeScript's benefits, convert your files as soon as
possible.

### Step 4: Gradual Typing

One of the strengths of TypeScript is that you don't have to
convert your entire codebase at once. TypeScript allows
for gradual typing. Begin by adding type annotations in
critical areas of your code, like function parameters,
return types, and object properties. You can leverage
```

TypeScript's `any` type temporarily for areas where you aren't ready to specify more precise types.

For example:

```typescript
function calculateTotal(price: number, quantity: number): number { return price * quantity;

}
```

Step 5: Address Type Errors

As you migrate your JavaScript code to TypeScript, you'll likely encounter type errors. TypeScript will give you feedback on areas where type safety can be improved. Make a habit of addressing these as you go to progressively strengthen your type definitions.

Step 6: Integrate Type Definitions

People often rely on third-party libraries that may not have built-in TypeScript definitions. You can install type declaration files from the DefinitelyTyped repository, which can be done with the following command:

```bash
npm install --save-dev @types/library-name
```

Replace `library-name` with the actual package name. If type definitions don't exist, you can create your own by defining a `.d.ts` file or using the `declare module` syntax.

Step 7: Testing

Migrate your test files similarly, ensuring all tests work as expected. Tools like Jest and Mocha have TypeScript support, so you can continue testing throughout the migration. Review your test configurations to ensure they're set up to handle TypeScript.

Step 8: Setup Linting and Formatting Tools

Linting tools like ESLint and Prettier can help enforce code style and catch common issues. Install the necessary packages for TypeScript support:

```bash
npm install --save-dev eslint @typescript-eslint/parser @typescript-eslint/eslint-plugin prettier
```

Create an ESLint configuration file and customize it to work with TypeScript.

By following the steps outlined in this chapter and embracing TypeScript's features, you'll prepare your project not only for current development challenges but also for future scalability and collaboration. A well-planned migration empowers developers and fosters a culture of writing clean, reliable, and self- documenting code.

Chapter 10: Modules and Namespaces in TypeScript

One of the key areas where TypeScript shines is in the organization and structuring of code, particularly through the use of modules and namespaces. This chapter will explore how modules and namespaces can help manage complexity and improve maintainability in TypeScript applications.

11.1 Understanding Modules

Modules are a fundamental building block of modern JavaScript and TypeScript applications. They allow developers to encapsulate code into distinct units, making it easier to manage dependencies, share code, and maintain a clean architecture. In TypeScript, a module is any file that contains `import` or `export` statements.

11.1.1 Creating a Module

To create a module in TypeScript, you simply create a new file and add `export` statements for the values, functions, classes, or interfaces you want to expose. For instance, let's create a simple module for mathematical operations:

```typescript
// mathUtils.ts

export function add(a: number, b: number): number {
return a + b;
}

export function subtract(a: number, b: number): number {
return a - b;
}
```

```
```

In the above example, `add` and `subtract` functions are exported from the `mathUtils.ts` module. ### 11.1.2 Importing a Module

To use functions from a module, you need to import them in another file. You can import specific items or the entire module using the `import` statement:

```typescript
// app.ts
import { add, subtract } from './mathUtils';
console.log(add(5, 3)); // Output: 8
console.log(subtract(5, 3)); // Output: 2
```

You can also use `import * as` syntax to import everything from a module under a single namespace:

```typescript
import * as MathUtils from './mathUtils';
console.log(MathUtils.add(5, 3)); // Output: 8
console.log(MathUtils.subtract(5, 3)); // Output: 2
```

11.1.3 Default Exports

TypeScript also supports default exports, enabling you to export a single item (function, class, etc.) from a module. The following example illustrates a default export:

```typescript
```

```typescript
// calculator.ts
export default class Calculator {
add(a: number, b: number): number { return a + b;
}
}
```

You can import it as follows:
```typescript
// app.ts
import Calculator from './calculator';
const calc = new Calculator(); console.log(calc.add(5, 3));
// Output: 8
```

11.2 Namespaces in TypeScript

Namespaces are a way to organize code in TypeScript by grouping related functionalities under a single identifier. They are particularly useful in situations where you want to avoid naming collisions and encapsulate functionalities together. However, it's important to note that after the introduction of ES6 modules, the use of namespaces has decreased. That said, they can still be helpful in certain scenarios.

11.2.1 Creating a Namespace

To create a namespace, use the `namespace` keyword, followed by a name. Here's how to define a namespace for the `MathUtils`:

```typescript namespace MathUtils {

export function add(a: number, b: number): number {
return a + b;

}

export function subtract(a: number, b: number): number {
return a - b;

}

}
```

11.2.2 Using a Namespace

You can call functions from a namespace by prefixing them with the namespace name:

```typescript
console.log(MathUtils.add(5, 3)); // Output: 8

console.log(MathUtils.subtract(5, 3)); // Output: 2
```

11.2.3 Nested Namespaces

Namespaces can also be nested, which can help further organize related functionalities:

```typescript namespace Geometry {

export namespace Shapes { export class Circle {

constructor(public radius: number) {}

area(): number {

return Math.PI * this.radius * this.radius;
```

```
}
    }
  }
}
```

// Using the nested namespace

```
const circle = new Geometry.Shapes.Circle(5);
console.log(circle.area()); // Output: 78.53981633974483
```
```

## 11.3 Modules vs. Namespaces

It's crucial to understand the differences between modules and namespaces when structuring your applications:

**Modules** work well for larger applications that are composed of many independent files. They are the recommended approach for organizing code in modern TypeScript applications, especially with the rising popularity of ES6 modules.


**Namespaces** can be helpful for smaller applications or when you want to group related code together without creating multiple files.

In general, it's advisable to favor modules, as they are compatible with various tools and libraries, promote better encapsulation, and lead to cleaner code.

## 11.4 Best Practices

When working with modules and namespaces in TypeScript, consider the following best practices:
```

Keep Modules Small: Each module should have a single responsibility. This makes them easier to manage and test.

Use Descriptive Names: Name your modules and namespaces clearly to reflect their purpose.

Prefer Modules Over Namespaces: With modern JavaScript and TypeScript, prefer using modules for code organization and dependency management.

Manage Dependencies Explicitly: Use `import` and `export` to manage dependencies clearly.

Avoid Global Exports: When using namespaces, be careful to limit the amount of global state to prevent conflicts.

Understanding how to leverage both features allows developers to write clean, maintainable, and scalable applications. As you continue to explore TypeScript, keep practicing the art of structuring your projects, and reap the benefits of clear and organized code.

Understanding ES Modules and TypeScript Modules

This chapter delves into the intricacies of ES (ECMAScript) Modules and TypeScript Modules, exploring their syntax, functionality, and how they interplay to create a robust development environment.

1. Introduction to Modules

Modules are self-contained pieces of code that

encapsulate functionality. They enable developers to break down large codebases into smaller, manageable chunks, fostering a clear structure and separation of concerns. The introduction of ES Modules has standardized the way JavaScript handles modularity, making it easier to manage dependencies and integrate code across diverse projects.

1.1 What are ES Modules?

ECMAScript Modules, commonly known as ES Modules (ESM), were introduced in ECMAScript 2015 (ES6). They provide a native JavaScript way to work with modules and allow developers to export and import code across different files. This native support for module syntax—using `import` and `export`—has drastically improved the modular capabilities of JavaScript.

Key Features of ES Modules:

Static Structure: The import and export declarations in ES Modules are static; this means they are determined at compile time, enabling better optimization by the JavaScript engine.

Asynchronous Loading: ES Modules are designed to be loaded asynchronously, allowing for a non- blocking development experience that can significantly enhance performance, particularly in web applications.

Scope Isolation: Each module has its own scope, which prevents clashes of variable and function names between different modules.

Interoperability: ES Modules can seamlessly work with CommonJS, the module system that Node.js previously used, making the transition between module systems smoother.

1.2 The Syntax of ES Modules

The core syntax for using ES Modules revolves around two main keywords: `export` and `import`. #### Exporting Modules

There are two ways to export functionality from a module: named exports and default exports.

Named Exports: Allow a module to export multiple entities.

```javascript
// math.js

export const pi = 3.14; export function add(x, y) {

return x + y;

}
```

Default Exports: Allow a module to export a single entity.

```javascript
// calculator.js

export default function multiply(x, y) { return x * y;

}
```

Importing Modules

Importing syntax varies depending on whether you are importing named or default exports.

Importing Named Exports:

```javascript
// main.js
import { pi, add } from './math.js'; console.log(pi); // 3.14
console.log(add(2, 3)); // 5
```

Importing Default Exports:

```javascript
// main.js
import multiply from './calculator.js';
console.log(multiply(2, 3)); // 6
```

1.3 TypeScript Modules

TypeScript, as a superset of JavaScript, builds upon ES Modules while adding additional layers of type safety and tooling support. TypeScript Modules follow the same syntax as ES Modules but allow for the incorporation of types, making it an excellent choice for developing robust, large-scale applications.

Type Security and Interface

One of the standout features of TypeScript is its strong type system. Defining types for exported entities provides better documentation and ensures that the intended use of functions, classes, and objects is clear.

```typescript
// math.ts
```

```typescript
export const pi: number = 3.14;

export function add(x: number, y: number): number {
return x + y;
}

export interface Shape { area: () => number;

}
```

When importing TypeScript modules, the same ES Module syntax is used, but TypeScript offers additional features such as interfaces, generics, and type assertions.

```typescript
// main.ts

import { pi, add, Shape } from './math';

const circle: Shape = {

area: () => pi * 5 * 5, // considering a circle with a radius of 5

};

console.log(`Area of the circle: ${circle.area()}`); // Area of the circle: 78.5
```

Module Resolution in TypeScript

TypeScript features a powerful module resolution system, enabling developers to customize how modules are found and compiled. This system supports both relative and absolute paths, as well as package imports.

1.4 Best Practices for Using ES and TypeScript

Modules

To enhance the effectiveness of modules in JavaScript and TypeScript, consider the following best practices:

Use Named Exports When Possible: Named exports are generally considered more readable, making it easier for developers to understand what a module contains at a glance.

Group Related Functions/Classes: When exporting multiple functions or classes, group them logically to maintain clarity.

Prefer Default Exports for Libraries: Libraries often benefit from default exports, as they allow for cleaner import statements in consumer code.

Utilize Type Definitions in TypeScript: Leverage TypeScript's type definitions to create self- documenting code and catch errors early in the development process.

Organize Your Codebase: Structure your modules into directories that align with your application features to enhance navigability and manageability.

Keep Modules Focused: Each module should ideally have a single responsibility, adhering to the principles of modular design.

Understanding ES Modules and TypeScript Modules is crucial for modern web development. By adopting these modular approaches, developers can create applications that are not only easier to reason about and maintain but also improve the overall quality of codebases.

Working with Namespaces and Code Organization

In this chapter, we will explore what namespaces are, how to use them effectively, and other techniques for organizing code in TypeScript.

1. Understanding Namespaces ### 1.1 What are Namespaces?

Namespaces in TypeScript are a way to group related code together, preventing naming collisions and allowing for modular architecture. They help in logical separation of code and can contain classes, interfaces, functions, and variables.

1.2 Syntax of Namespaces

The basic syntax for creating a namespace in TypeScript involves using the `namespace` keyword followed by the namespace name. Here's an example:

```typescript
namespace MathUtilities {

export function add(a: number, b: number): number {
return a + b;
}


export function subtract(a: number, b: number): number {
return a - b;
}
}
```

```
```

In this example, we've created a `MathUtilities` namespace containing two functions: `add` and `subtract`. The `export` keyword is important because it allows these functions to be accessible outside the namespace.

1.3 Using Namespaces

To access functions or classes within a namespace, you simply reference them using the namespace name followed by a dot. Here's how you can call the functions defined earlier:

```typescript
let sum = MathUtilities.add(5, 3); // Outputs: 8

let difference = MathUtilities.subtract(10, 4); // Outputs: 6
```

1.4 Nested Namespaces

Namespaces can also be nested, which allows for even more granular organization. Here's an example of nested namespaces:

```typescript
namespace MyApp {

export namespace Utilities {

export function log(message: string): void {
console.log(message);

}

}
```

```
}
```

// Using the nested namespace

MyApp.Utilities.log("Hello from nested namespaces!"); // Outputs: Hello from nested namespaces!
```
` ` `
```

2. Organizing Code with Namespaces ### 2.1 Benefits of Using Namespaces Namespaces provide several advantages:

Avoid Name Collisions: In large applications, different modules may use the same names for classes or functions. Namespaces avoid conflicts by encapsulating these names.

Logical Grouping: Structuring related code into namespaces enhances readability and maintainability, making it clear where certain functionalities reside.

Encapsulation: Namespaces provide a way to define a logical encapsulation scope, allowing you to hide implementation details from the global scope.

2.2 Structuring a TypeScript Project

A well-structured TypeScript project typically involves organizing source code into directories that map to namespaces. For example, a project might be structured like this:

```
` ` ` src/
```

MathUtilities.ts StringUtilities.ts App.ts
```
` ` `
```

Each file could define its own namespace. For example, `MathUtilities.ts` could contain a `MathUtilities` namespace, while `StringUtilities.ts` could contain a `StringUtilities` namespace. This file-based organizational approach makes it easier to manage the codebase.

3. Combining Namespaces with Modules

While namespaces offer code encapsulation, TypeScript also supports modules, which allow for better code organization through file imports and exports. In modern applications, modules are often preferred over namespaces.

3.1 Using Modules

To define a module in TypeScript, you usually export classes, interfaces, or functions from a file. For example:

```typescript
// StringUtilities.ts

export function toUpperCase(str: string): string { return str.toUpperCase();

}


// App.ts

import { toUpperCase } from './StringUtilities';

console.log(toUpperCase('hello world')); // Outputs: HELLO WORLD
```

3.2 When to Use Namespaces vs. Modules

While both namespaces and modules have their uses, it's

important to know when to use each.

Namespaces: Best suited for legacy projects or when working within a single file where encapsulation is necessary without the overhead of module systems.

Modules: Preferred for new projects, providing clearer organization through imports and exports, facilitating better dependency management.

4. Best Practices for Code Organization

To maintain a clean and efficient codebase in TypeScript, consider the following best practices:

Use Descriptive Namespaces: Choose meaningful names for your namespaces to reflect their purpose.

Limit Scope Width: Avoid excessively broad namespaces; instead, keep functionalities focused and modular.

Think in Features, Not Files: When structuring your code, consider grouping by feature instead of file type. This leads to a more cohesive code organization.

Document Your Code: Always document your namespaces, classes, and functions to enhance understandability for future maintainers.

By leveraging both namespaces and modules appropriately, developers can craft a well-structured and clean codebase that is easier to navigate and maintain. Embrace these concepts as you continue your journey in TypeScript programming, fostering better code organization and organization methodologies.

Chapter 11: Error Handling and Debugging in TypeScript

In this chapter, we will explore these mechanisms in detail, providing practical examples to enhance your understanding.

11.1 Understanding Errors in TypeScript

Errors in TypeScript can generally be divided into two categories: **compile-time errors** and **runtime errors**.

11.1.1 Compile-time Errors

These errors occur during the compilation process when TypeScript checks your code against its type system. Common examples include type mismatches, undeclared variables, and incorrect function signatures. The TypeScript compiler provides detailed error messages that help you identify and resolve these issues before execution.

Example of a Compile-time Error:

```typescript
function add(a: number, b: number): number { return a + b;
}

console.log(add(10, '20')); // Compile-time error: Argument of type 'string' is not assignable to parameter of type 'number'.
```

11.1.2 Runtime Errors

Unlike compile-time errors, runtime errors occur during the execution of the program. These can be caused by a variety of issues such as null references, out-of-bounds access, or unexpected user input. Handling these errors is crucial for creating robust applications that maintain functionality even in the face of unforeseen circumstances.

Example of a Runtime Error:

```typescript
function getUser(id: number): string { const users = { 1: 'Alice', 2: 'Bob' };

return users[id]; // Runtime error if id is not in the users object.
}

console.log(getUser(3)); // Output: undefined
```

11.2 Error Handling with Try-Catch

TypeScript supports traditional error handling via the `try-catch` mechanism. This allows you to gracefully handle runtime errors without crashing your application. When an error occurs within the `try` block, control is passed to the `catch` block, where you can manage the error accordingly.

11.2.1 Using Try-Catch

```typescript
function parseJSON(json: string) { try {

return JSON.parse(json);

} catch (error) {
```

```
console.error('Parse Error:', error);
```

return null; // Returning null is one way to handle the error.

```
}
}
```

const data = parseJSON('{"name": "Alice"}'); console.log(data); // Output: { name: 'Alice' }

const invalidData = parseJSON('{"name": "Alice"'); // Invalid JSON console.log(invalidData); // Output: Parse Error: SyntaxError: Unexpected end of JSON input

```
```

11.2.2 Error Types

In the `catch` block, the error can be typed to provide better insights into the nature of the error.

```typescript
try {
```

// code that may throw an error

```
} catch (error) {
```

if (error instanceof SyntaxError) {

// Handle syntax errors specifically

```
} else {
```

// Handle generic errors

```
}
}
```
```

## 11.3 Custom Error Handling
```

Creating custom error classes allows you to define specific error types that can convey detailed information about the issues that arise within your application. This practice enhances error management by providing more contextual data.

11.3.1 Creating a Custom Error Class

```typescript
class CustomError extends Error { constructor(message: string) {

super(message);

this.name = 'CustomError'; // Setting the name of the error

}

}

function doSomething() {

throw new CustomError('Something went wrong!');

}

try {

doSomething();

} catch (error) {

if (error instanceof CustomError) {

console.error(error.name + ': ' + error.message); // CustomError: Something went wrong!

}

}
```

```

```

11.4 Debugging TypeScript Applications

Debugging TypeScript applications can be effectively managed using various tools and practices. TypeScript, being a superset of JavaScript, can utilize existing JavaScript debugging tools and techniques with some additional features that benefit type safety.

11.4.1 Source Maps

Source maps play a vital role in debugging TypeScript. They map the TypeScript code to the JavaScript code that gets executed, allowing developers to debug the original TypeScript instead of the transpiled JavaScript. This is especially useful for identifying the location of errors in your TypeScript files directly.

To enable source maps, adjust your `tsconfig.json`:

```json
{

"compilerOptions": { "sourceMap": true

}

}
```

11.4.2 Using Debuggers

Most modern development environments, such as Visual Studio Code, come with built-in debugging tools. These allow you to set breakpoints, inspect variables, and step through your TypeScript code line by line.

Setting Up Debugging in Visual Studio Code

169

Open your project in Visual Studio Code.

Go to the Debug view.

Click on the gear icon to configure your `launch.json`.

Add a configuration to launch your TypeScript application.
Example of a Basic Launch Configuration

```json
{
"version": "0.2.0", "configurations": [
{
"type": "node",
"request": "launch", "name": "Launch Program",
"program":          "${workspaceFolder}/dist/index.js",
"outFiles":          ["${workspaceFolder}/dist/**/*.js"],
"sourceMaps": true
}
]
}
```

11.5 Best Practices for Error Handling and Debugging

Always Use Try-Catch: For critical sections of code that may fail, always encapsulate them in try- catch blocks.

Be Specific with Error Handling: Use specific error types in your catch blocks to handle known error scenarios differently.

Use Custom Errors: Create custom error classes for domain-specific errors to provide more context in error handling.

Log Errors: Use logging mechanisms to log errors, stack traces, and contextual information to help in diagnosing issues.

Leverage Type Checks: Type guards can help prevent runtime errors by ensuring variables conform to expected types before usage.

Employ Unit Tests: Writing tests can help catch many errors at compile time and identify potential issues before they reach production.

Understanding the differences between compile-time and runtime errors, and mastering the various mechanisms for handling them will significantly enhance your development experience.

Using Try-Catch and Custom Errors

In TypeScript, an extension of JavaScript that adds type safety to the language, error handling can be efficiently managed using `try-catch` statements and custom errors. This chapter explores how developers can effectively utilize these tools to create robust applications.

Understanding Try-Catch

The `try-catch` statement is used to handle exceptions that may occur in code. The `try` block contains code that might throw an error, while the `catch` block allows you to handle that error gracefully. This mechanism is essential for maintaining program stability and providing meaningful feedback to the user.

Basic Syntax

Here's a simple example of the `try-catch` statement in TypeScript:

```typescript
function potentiallyFailingOperation() {

throw new Error("Something went wrong!");

}

try {

potentiallyFailingOperation();

} catch (error) {

console.error("An error occurred:", error.message);

}
```

In the example, the `potentiallyFailingOperation` function throws an error. When we call this function within the `try` block, control is passed to the `catch` block upon encountering the error. This allows us to log the error message rather than crashing the entire application.

Catching Specific Errors

TypeScript allows for more granular error handling. You can catch specific error types, particularly those that extend the built-in `Error` class. This approach can be useful for distinguishing different error conditions.

```typescript
```

```
class CustomError extends Error { constructor(message:
string) {
super(message);
this.name = "CustomError";
}
}
function riskyOperation() {
throw new CustomError("A custom error occurred!");
}
try {
riskyOperation();
} catch (error) {
if (error instanceof CustomError) {
console.error("Caught a custom error:", error.message);
} else {
console.error("An unexpected error occurred:", error);
}
}
```
```

Here, we defined a `CustomError` class that extends the
built-in `Error` class. In the catch block, we used the

`instanceof` operator to determine whether the caught
error is a `CustomError`. This allows for tailored handling
of specific error types.
```

Creating Custom Errors

Custom errors can significantly enhance error handling in your applications by providing additional context and specificity. In TypeScript, creating custom errors involves extending the base `Error` class and adding any properties or methods necessary for your application's needs.

Defining a Custom Error

Let's define a custom error that includes an error code:

```typescript
class ValidationError extends Error { public code: number;

constructor(message: string, code: number) { super(message);

this.code = code;

this.name = "ValidationError";

}

}
```

In this `ValidationError` class, we added a `code` property that can be used to indicate specific validation issues. This property can be particularly useful for clients consuming your APIs or services.

Using Custom Errors

You can throw and catch the `ValidationError` as follows:

```typescript
```

```
function validateInput(input: any) { if (!input) {
throw new ValidationError("Input cannot be empty",
400);
}
}
try {
validateInput(null);
} catch (error) {
if (error instanceof ValidationError) {
console.error(`Validation failed: ${error.message} (Code:
${error.code})`);
}
}
```
```

This example shows how to validate an input and throw a
`ValidationError` if the input is invalid. The custom error
can carry additional information, providing clarity about
the nature of the failure.

## Best Practices for Error Handling

When using `try-catch` and custom errors in TypeScript,
consider the following best practices:

**Use Specific Error Types:** Create specific error classes
to represent different error conditions. This helps
differentiate between issues and provides more context for
handling them.

**Don't Overuse Try-Catch:** Use `try-catch` only
```

around code that is likely to throw exceptions. Overusing it can lead to cluttered code and obscure error handling logic.

Log Errors Thoughtfully: When catching and logging errors, include as much relevant information as possible to assist with debugging without exposing sensitive information. Capture stack traces and other context-specific details where appropriate.

Graceful Degradation: Ensure that your application remains usable even when errors occur. Provide users with meaningful feedback and options to recover from errors.

Re-throw Errors if Necessary: If you cannot handle an error appropriately at a certain level, consider re-throwing it. This gives higher-level functions the opportunity to catch it and handle it accordingly.

```typescript
try {
riskyFunction();
} catch (error) {
// Handle specific error
throw error; // Re-throwing the error to the caller
}
```

Effective error handling is an essential skill for any TypeScript developer. Utilizing `try-catch` statements and custom errors allows you to build applications that are not only robust but also user-friendly. By understanding the nuances of error handling and incorporating best practices into your workflows, you can significantly enhance your application's resilience against failures and improve the overall developer experience.

Debugging TypeScript Code with VS Code

Debugging is an essential skill for any developer, and when it comes to TypeScript—a superset of JavaScript that adds static typing to the language—the process can be straightforward and efficient, especially using Visual Studio Code (VS Code). In this chapter, we will explore how to effectively set up and utilize debugging tools available in VS Code to troubleshoot and refine your TypeScript applications.

1. Setting Up Your TypeScript Environment

Before diving into debugging, ensure that your TypeScript environment is set up correctly. You will need:

Node.js: Make sure Node.js is installed on your machine, as it is necessary for running TypeScript code outside the browser.

TypeScript Compiler: You can install TypeScript globally via npm with the following command:

```bash
npm install -g typescript
```

VS Code: Download and install Visual Studio Code, if you haven't already. It comes with built-in support for JavaScript and TypeScript.

Once you have the necessary tools, create a new

TypeScript project and initialize it with a `tsconfig.json` file:

```bash
mkdir my-typescript-project cd my-typescript-project

tsc --init
```

This command will create a basic TypeScript configuration file that you can modify as needed. ## 2. Writing Sample TypeScript Code

For the purpose of debugging, let's create a simple TypeScript file. Create a file named `app.ts` and add the following code:

```typescript
function add(a: number, b: number): number { return a + b;
}

function greet(name: string): string { return `Hello, ${name}!`;
}

const result = add(5, "10"); console.log(greet("World"));
console.log(result);
```

In this code snippet, you may notice an intentional error where a number and a string are being added together. We'll use this for debugging.

3. Configuring Launch Settings

VS Code uses a configuration file named `launch.json` to define how the debugger should run your application. To create this configuration, follow these steps:

Open the Debug view by clicking the Debug icon on the Activity Bar on the left side of the window or by pressing `Ctrl+Shift+D`.

Click on the gear icon to configure a new launch.json file.

Choose "Node.js" when prompted.

Here is an example of what your `launch.json` might look like:

```json
{
"version": "0.2.0", "configurations": [
{
"type": "node",
"request": "launch", "name": "Launch Program",
"program":                    "${workspaceFolder}/app.js",
"preLaunchTask": "tsc: build - tsconfig.json", "outFiles":
["${workspaceFolder}/**/*.js"]
}
]
}
```

Note:

- Ensure `outFiles` points to the location of the compiled JavaScript files from the TypeScript source files. ## 4.
179

Building TypeScript Files

Before debugging, you need to compile your TypeScript files to JavaScript. You can do this using the TypeScript compiler:

```bash tsc
```

Alternatively, you can set up a watch mode that automatically compiles files when saved. Run the command:

```bash

tsc --watch
```

5. Adding Breakpoints

Now that you have your environment set up, you can start debugging. Open `app.ts` in VS Code and:

Click in the gutter next to a line number where you want to add a breakpoint (e.g., on the line `const result

= add(5, "10");`).

You should see a red dot indicating a breakpoint has been set. ## 6. Starting the Debugger

With your breakpoints in place, follow these steps to start debugging:

Select the run and debug configuration you created in the Debug view.

Click the green play button (or press `F5`) to start debugging.

The VS Code debugger will start, and execution will pause at your breakpoint. You can now use various debugging tools to inspect your code.

7. Debugging Tools in VS Code

While the debugger is paused, you have access to several tools:

Debug Console: This allows you to evaluate expressions and inspect values.

Variables Panel: View the current state of variables and their values.

Call Stack Panel: Understand the stack of function calls that led to the current breakpoint.

Watch Panel: Add specific variables or expressions to watch during the debugging session. ### Navigating Your Code

You can control the execution flow using the following options:

Continue (F5): Resumes program execution until the next breakpoint.

Step Over (F10): Executes the next line of code, but does not step into functions.

Step Into (F11): Steps into the function calls to debug.

Step Out (Shift + F11): Exits the current function and returns to the caller. ## 8. Identifying and Fixing Issues

With the debugger tools, you can inspect the types being passed to the `add` function and notice that a string is being passed instead of a number. Update your code as follows to ensure type safety:

```typescript
const result = add(5, Number("10")); // Convert string to
number
```

With this fix, you can rerun the debugger and confirm that the application functions as expected.

By utilizing breakpoints, stepping through code, and inspecting variable states, you can quickly rectify errors and improve your code quality. Practice these techniques as you develop your TypeScript applications, and you will find that the debugging process becomes an invaluable aspect of your coding toolkit.

Conclusion

As we reach the end of this guide, we hope that you have gained a solid understanding of TypeScript and its role in modern web development. By now, you should be well-equipped with the foundational concepts of TypeScript, its advantages over JavaScript, and practical applications that can elevate your coding experience.

TypeScript is not just a superset of JavaScript; it is a powerful tool that enhances your coding efficiency, promotes better software design, and fosters collaboration among developers. Its static typing, rich tooling, and improved readability will not only help you write more reliable and maintainable code but also position you well for future projects in an ever-evolving tech landscape.

As you continue your journey with TypeScript, we encourage you to practice regularly, experiment with different scenarios, and delve deeper into advanced features such as generics, decorators, and utility types. Participate in the vibrant TypeScript community—attend meetups, follow experts, and contribute to open- source projects. The more you engage with TypeScript, the more proficient you will become.

Remember, your learning journey doesn't stop here. The field of web development is constantly changing, and there's always more to explore. Keep up-to-date with the latest features in TypeScript, best practices in software development, and emerging tools that can enhance your workflow.

In conclusion, TypeScript is not merely a trend; it is an integral step into the future of JavaScript development. Empower yourself with the knowledge you've gained, and take the next step in your programming career with confidence. We wish you the best of luck on your journey as a TypeScript developer, and we can't wait to see what you create!

Biography

Adriam Miller is a passionate technologist, web development expert, and the visionary mind behind groundbreaking digital solutions. With a deep-rooted love for **TypeScript programming, web development, and cutting-edge web applications**, Adriam has dedicated his career to transforming ideas into dynamic, high-performance digital experiences.

Driven by an insatiable curiosity and a commitment to innovation, Adriam's expertise spans across front-end and back-end development, harnessing the power of modern technologies to build scalable and efficient web applications. His ability to **simplify complex concepts and turn them into actionable insights** makes his work not only powerful but also accessible to developers and entrepreneurs alike.

Beyond coding, Adriam is an advocate for **continuous learning and sharing knowledge**, believing that the digital world thrives when creators push boundaries and explore new possibilities. Whether crafting seamless user interfaces, optimizing performance, or mentoring aspiring developers, his passion for the web shines through in every project he undertakes.

In this book, Adriam distills his **years of experience, practical know-how, and innovative mindset** into a comprehensive guide that empowers readers to **master Miller** and elevate their development skills to new heights. If you're ready to unlock your full potential in web development, you're in the right place—Adriam Miller is here to guide you on the journey.

Glossary: TypeScript for beginners

1. TypeScript

TypeScript is a statically typed superset of JavaScript that compiles to plain JavaScript. It allows developers to add type annotations to their code, enabling better tooling, error checking, and more robust software development.

2. Static Typing

Static typing refers to the method of defining variable

types at compile time rather than at runtime. This allows for earlier detection of potential errors and makes the code easier to understand and maintain.

3. Type Annotations

Type annotations are syntactic constructs that specify the data type of a variable, parameter, or return value. In TypeScript, you can explicitly define the type of a variable using a colon followed by the type name, as in

`let age: number = 30;`.

4. Interface

An interface in TypeScript defines a contract for the structure of an object. It specifies which properties and methods an object should have but does not provide the implementation.

5. Class

A class is a blueprint for creating objects in object-oriented programming. In TypeScript, classes can have properties, methods, and constructors. TypeScript supports concepts like inheritance, encapsulation, and polymorphism.

6. Module

Modules in TypeScript are files that contain code encapsulated in their own scope. They can export functionalities (functions, classes, variables) that can be imported and used in other modules. This helps in organizing and structuring code effectively.

7. Compilation

Compilation is the process of converting TypeScript code into plain JavaScript code. TypeScript is compiled either via the command line or through build tools, enabling the resulting JavaScript to run in any environment that supports JavaScript.

8. Type Inference

Type inference is a feature of TypeScript that automatically determines the type of a variable based on its assigned value. For example, if you write `let message = "Hello, World!";`, TypeScript infers that `message` is of type `string`.

9. Union Types

Union types allow a variable to hold values of multiple types. This is useful for functions that can accept different data types. An example of a union type is:

```typescript
let value: string | number;
```

10. Generics

Generics are a way to create reusable code components that can work with different data types. By using generics, developers can define a function or class that can operate on various types while ensuring type safety.

11. Enums

Enums (short for Enumerations) are a special "class" that represents a group of constants. This allows for better readability and maintainability in code.

12. Any Type

The `any` type is a way to opt-out of type checking in TypeScript. It allows a variable to have any type, which can be useful in scenarios where the type is not known at compile time, but it also defeats the purpose of using TypeScript for type safety.

13. Tuple

A tuple is a special type of array that can hold a fixed number of elements with specific types. They are useful for representing data structures with known, but potentially varied, data types. For example:

```typescript
let person: [string, number] = ["Alice", 30];
```

14. Type Guard

Type guards are mechanisms used to narrow down the type of a variable within a conditional block. They help the TypeScript compiler understand the type of a variable at runtime, thus enabling better type checking and error prevention.

15. Decorators

Decorators are special annotations that can be applied to classes, methods, or properties to modify their behavior in a clean and reusable way. They are often used in frameworks such as Angular for dependency injection and defining routes.

www.ingramcontent.com/pod-product-compliance
Lightning Source LLC
LaVergne TN
LVHW051334050326
832903LV00031B/3531